SUNFLOWERS

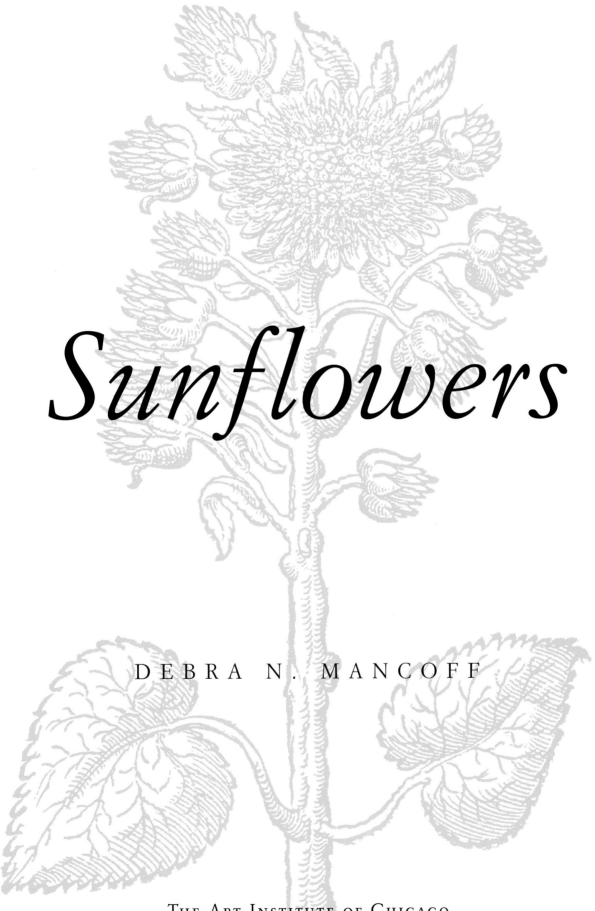

Sunflowers

DEBRA N. MANCOFF

THE ART INSTITUTE OF CHICAGO

Thames & Hudson

Published in association with The Art Institute of Chicago
Copyright © 2001 by The Art Institute of Chicago

First published in hardcover in the United States of America
in 2001 by Thames & Hudson Inc., 500 Fifth Avenue, New
York, New York 10110

First published in the United Kingdom in 2001 by Thames &
Hudson Ltd, 181A High Holborn, London WC1V 7QX

Library of Congress Catalog Card Number 2001087385

British Library Cataloguing-in-Publication data
A catalogue record for this book is available from the
British Library

ISBN 0-500-51053-9

Edited by Susan F. Rossen, Executive Director of
  Publications, The Art Institute of Chicago
Photography editor: Carol Parden, Chicago
Designed by Joan Sommers Design, Chicago
Production by Amanda W. Freymann, Associate Director of
  Publications-Production, and Stacey Hendricks, Production
  Assistant

Printed and bound in Singapore by Tien Wah Press

First edition

Front cover: CLOCKWISE FROM TOP LEFT Bosschaert (p. 38);
  van Gogh (p. 94); Holtzbecker (p. 33); van Dyke (p. 44)
  BELOW Mattioli (p. 30)
Endsheets: de Morgan (p. 70)
Frontispiece: ABOVE Jeckyll (p. 74) BELOW, LEFT TO RIGHT,
  Holtzbecker (p. 33); van Gogh (p. 88); Morris (p. 74)
Title page: Mattioli (p. 30)
Contents: PAGE 4 From Claude Paradin and Gabriele
  Simeoni, *Les Dévises héroiques. . .*, 1561, woodcut; Besler
  (p. 16); Causé (p. 23); anonymous (p. 37) PAGE 5 de Morgan
  (p. 70); van Gogh (pp. 92–93); Paradin and Simeoni (see
  above)
Back cover: LEFT TOP TO BOTTOM de Heem (p. 8); Besler
  (p. 28); van Gogh (pp. 92–93); Hayllar (p. 68) RIGHT Mattioli
  (p. 30)

"The sunflower is
mine in a way."

VINCENT VAN GOGH

Letter to Theo van Gogh, 1889

Georges Monzana-Pissarro, *Frame with Sunflowers*, 1889, stamped brass

In a letter to his brother Theo, written in the fall of 1888, Vincent van Gogh described the charming features of a guest room in his Yellow House in Arles. "In the morning, when you open the window, you will see the green of the gardens and the rising sun, and the road into town. But you will see these great pictures of the sunflowers, 12 or 14 to the bunch, crammed into this tiny boudoir with its pretty bed and everything else dainty. It will not be commonplace."

Van Gogh had begun his series of bouquets that August, hoping to complete at least one dozen canvases before the summer ended and the sunflowers faded. The palette he selected—yellows and golds, blues and greens—reflected his long fascination with the visual effects of complimentary colors. His original plan was to hang the ensemble in his studio, but as he worked, his subject gained a deep, personal dimension. The vibrant colors, radiant blooms, and

OPPOSITE LEFT, TOP TO BOTTOM, Sweerts (p. 17), Besler (p. 16), de Passe (p. 29), Miller (p. 31) OPPOSITE RIGHT Jan Davidsz de Heem, *Fruit and Flowers with Eucharistic Wine*, 1651, oil on canvas ABOVE van Gogh (p. 88)

vigorous, sturdy stalks came to embody the force that ignited one of van Gogh's most inspired and energetic periods of painting: the heat and vitality of the Provençal sun. Perhaps, his desire to share his appreciation of nature's revitalizing power prompted the artist to place the sunflower images in the guest room rather than in his studio. The paintings offered his guests a gift of everlasting sum-

mer, a golden tribute to the glories of the southern sun.

More than a century later, the brightly painted bouquets endure as the icon of a passionate artist whose love of nature was a constant source of inspiration and affirmation. The sunflower compositions reign as the most popular and most recognizable subject van Gogh painted. From commercial advertisements to the Dutch gilder note, from posters and cards to coffee mugs and museum-shop souvenirs, sunflowers are reproduced in an imaginative array, and through the ongoing demand for these images and items millions of people honor the artist.

Yet van Gogh's association with the sunflower came late to a flower with a long and varied history. Cultivated in the western hemisphere for more than five thousand years, the sunflower was unknown in Europe until the early sixteenth century. Prior to that time, naturalists observed the response of certain flowers to the daily course of the sun, turning—as if in constant worship—from east at dawn to west at dusk. These "sunflowers," whose motions paid homage to the sun's rays, came to signify ultimate devotion. With its vibrant color and solar shape, the sunflower of the Americas inherited this rich, symbolic tradition, fusing botanical knowledge and floral lore. Over the centuries, the sunflower has appeared as the attribute of ardent lover, loyal courtier, faithful spouse, and pious soul. Like the sunflower basking in the sun, each faithful

ABOVE E. Kychicus, *Helianthus*, 1703, colored engraving BELOW Eugène Grasset, *La Grande Dame*, cover for *Revue de l'élégance et de l'art*, 1895, color lithograph

follower drew strength from the object of its homage; the act of devotion became both a source of vitality and a reason for existence. The story of the sunflower neither begins nor ends with Vincent van Gogh, but his paintings open the door to the meaningful legacy of his signature flower. Later in his life, van Gogh would modestly declare, "The sunflower is mine in a way," but he remained true to the flower's tradition, taking it not as a personal emblem, but as a symbol of constancy, gratitude, and love.

ALL CHRISTMASTIDE MAY JOY ABIDE!

ABOVE William de Morgan, *Sunflower Tile*, 1880s, glazed earthenware BELOW Georgina Koberwein Terrell, *Christmas Card*, c. 1880 OPPOSITE TOP, LEFT TO RIGHT. de Morgan (p. 70); Kihō (p. 76); van Gogh (pp. 92–93), Mondrian (p. 105) OPPOSITE BELOW Yasuhiro Ishimoto, *Common Sunflower*, 1986–87, photograph

¶ Albericus vespuciius Laurentio petri Francisci vil grues mit glücklicher fart/am vierzehenden tag des monatz may thausent fünffhundert ein jar schieden wir
von Olisippo nach gebot des obgenantē künigs mit dreyē schyffen zuersüchē Newe landt vñ Jnsell gegemittagvō sind also hin vñ her geschiffet mit grosser vn-
gestümigkeyt des meres biß auff den sibendē tag des monats Augusto/des obgemeltē jars gesindē ein grosses Landt vñ Reygiō/vñ so grosse volcker/scharen vñ
leüt/dz die nyemant erzelē mocht als man list in Apocalpsis/Ein volck sach ich/ein mildt güetig vñ hantweysig/vñ gend all nackent/beyde weyß vñ man/vnnd
gantz on bedeckung jrer leibe an alle enden/wie sie auß muter leib kumē/also gend sie biß sie sterbē/dan sie sind groß võ leib vierschrötig/wol geschickt güter schön
er glidmaß vñ geferbt etlicher maß gegē rotem/das ich mein dise võ vrsach kume das sie nackēt gond vñ von der sunē bescheine/also geferbt werde sie haben weit
vñ groß harlöck vñ schwartz sie sind in jrē gang vñ mit spil treibē thetig vñ gering/vñ gütiger vñ schoner antlitze die sie doch jne selbs heßlich machē vñ vngestalt
dan sie poē jnen selbs löcher in die packē/die mundleffzē vñ die nasen vñ die oren.Du solt auch nit gedenckē dz solche löcher klein sein/ob sie eins allein habē dan ich
etlich gesehē hab die in jrem antlytz allein sibē löcher/der yeglichs so groß was das ein kriech od haselnus wol in eins gen möcht/sie vstossen jne selbs solche löcher
mit plabē steinē/Cristallē/Marmor vñ Alabaster gar hübsch vñ schön/vnnd mit weyssen gebein/vñ mit andern dinge/so mit künstē gemacht werde/nach jrer
gewonheit/Vnd ob du also sehest ein so sreind vngewont ding/so mit grossem selzamē vwundunge/ Viemlich einen menschē der do het in dē backen/allein vñ in
den leffzen/siben stein d etlicher ir in der leng einer halbē span/du würdest nit on grosse vwundung sein. Danich hab dick wargenumē vñ vber scherzt/dz sibē solch
er stein am gewicht habē.xvj.lot vber/vñ on das sie in dē oren/die mit dreyen löcheren durch stochē sind/sie noch ander stein tragē/die in ringen hange vñ dise weiß
vñ sitte ist allein der manē/dan die frawen zerstechē jnen selbs ir antlytz nit also mit löcherung/dan allein ir oren. Ein ander sitt vñ weiß/ist auch vnd vñ bey jnē genueg abweysig/vñ wider alle menschliche glaubung. Das ir frawē die eben gelüstig vñ gayl sind/vñ tri manē machen das jnen ire mendliche glit geschwellen in
solcher vber dick das sie vngestalt vñ schmelich erscheinē/vñ das thon sie mit etliche gifftigē thierlen/vnd võ solcher sach geschicht dz inen vil ir gemecht vderben
die in von mangels wege der arzeney saule/vnd beleiben on gemecht. Sie habē kein tuech noch deck/weder leines noch baumwolles/dan sie es nit bedürffen vñ
habē kein aygen gut. Sunder alle ding seind vnder jnen gemein/sie habē auch keinen künig oder regierer. Sunder ein yeder ist im selbs ein herr/souil weiber nemen
sie so vil sie wöllē/vñ der sun mit d mutter/vñ der bruder mit d schwester/vñ der erst mit d ersten/vñ der begegner mit der begegnerin. Vnd veinigen sich als dick
als sie wöllē/scheide sie die ee vñ halltē gantz kein ordenung/darumb haben sie auch keinen tempel vñ halltē kein gesatz/vñ seind nit abgötter. Was soll ich mer sage
sie leben nach der natur dz siewol Epicuri bauch füller genant werdē mügen dan Senici. Bey jnen seind kein kaufleüt noch kauffmans güet. Die scharē des volcks
haben auch krieg vñ an kunst vñ ordnung/jre eltern mit jren rethen vñ geboten die junge zuthon was sie wöllē/vñ rüsten sich zustreytē/ Jn solchen
sie einand grausamlich zu tod schlahen/vñ welche sie also im krieg vñ streit fahen die füren sie hin/domit sie die bey lebē lassen/vñ sie behaltē das sie dar võ mestig
en vñ sie essen dan einer den andern der do obligt/vñ vnder andern fleysch ist yr menschē fleysch ein speyß/ Es hat der vater sein sun vñ sein weyb gessen ich hab
einē gesehen von dem sagt man er het wol von dreyhundert menschē leybē geessen/ich bin gewesen an einem end da hab ich gesehen gesalzen menschē fleysch vñ
auff gehenckt zu derren/wie hie bey vns das schweine fleysch/sie verwundn sich warumb wir vnser veint fleysch nit auch essen in vnser speyß/dan sie meinē dz es
das aller beste fleysch sey/ir waffen seind pogē vñ pfeyl vñ wen sie streiten/so bedeckē sie sich nit/Wir rieten in von solcher pöser weyß zulassen/vñ sie vhiesen vns
dar von zulassen/vñ ob die frawē schön ploß vñ nacket gend/so haben sie doch ir leib hübsch vñ wol gestalt vñ sauber vñ send nit so schentlich als einer gedenckē
möcht wan sie genueg leibig seind/so wirt ir scham nindert gesehen vns nan wund das vnder inen keine gesehen ward die do lampend prüst het oder die gekindet
heten dz der selben bauch anderst gestalt werde dan d junckfrwē vñ die nie gekindet/vñ on andern glidern vñ enden des leybs d gleichē vmerckt ward/das ich
alles von ersamkeit weyter vngeendert laß/dan wan sie sich möchten zu den Cristen menschē gefiegen als sie auß der massen gayl sind/so legtē sie alle scham võ in
zu volbringē böse werck. Sie leben hundert vñ fünffzig jar vñ werden seltē kranck/vñ ob sie etwan kranck werdē so heylen sie sich selber mit wurtzeln/vñ mit güetē

Solas Indianus

Tall and stately, with its radiant petals encircling a dark disk, the sunflower seems aptly named. The great Swedish naturalist Carolus Linneaus identified the genus of the common annual sunflower as *Helianthus annuus*, a Greek compound based on *helios* (the sun) and *anthos* (a flower), in his taxonomy of plants, *Systema Naturae* (1735). He cited the plant's spectacular appearance as his inspiration, exclaiming: "Who can see this plant in flower, whose great golden blossoms send out rays in every direction from the circular disk, without admiring the handsome flower modelled on the sun's shape?" Yet long before Linneaus created his nomenclature, the sunflower grew wild across the broad plains of the western hemisphere. It was unknown in Europe until the decades after the Columbian encounter of the late fifteenth century with what would come to be known as the Americas; the first botanical names that introduced the "new-world" plant to the "old"—"The Golden Flower of Peru," "The Hearbe of the Sunne," "Solas indianus"—hint at the sunflower's storied past.

While the written history of the sunflower originated in Europe, archaeological evidence reveals that the plant, both wild and cultivated, was long integral to the life of the early inhabitants

I.

Flos Solis prolifer.

of the Americas. Carbon dating estimates the age of a single, preserved achene (the so-called kernel of the central disk) from a site in modern-day Colorado to be five thousand years old. Other findings have included dried heads from Tularosa Cave in New Mexico, quarts of achenes from cultivated giant sunflowers in Ohio, and achenes an inch in length in North Dakota. The perishable nature of plant remains makes such findings rare, but the evidence that has survived, coupled with written observations in journals of European explorers, provides a vivid account of the sunflower's practical role in its native home.

The sunflower's natural habitat ranged across the eastern woodlands and the western plains from the Canadian border to northern Mexico. Whether gathered in the wild or cultivated, sunflowers served as a basic food plant for many North American tribes. In 1588, while traveling through the Pamlico Sound region of North Carolina, explorer Thomas Hariot took note of a "great herbe . . . about six foote in height" with a flower "a spanne in breath." He claimed that the Algonquian Indians made it into "bread and broth," and that the Choctaw mixed sunflower meal with ground maize to produce "a very palatable bread." In 1615 Samuel de Champlain remarked on its use by the

Huron; during their search for a land route west to the Pacific in 1803, Meriwether Lewis and William Clark observed that many tribes ground the seeds for meal.

Along with meal, ground achenes provided oil, which was used to flavor food and groom hair. Pigments were extracted from individual parts of the plant, and many tribes employed the petals, or ray flowers, to make a yellow dye. The Hopi soaked achenes in water to create a purple dye for basketry and body paint. The sunflower was also a valued medicinal plant. The Dakota people simmered the heads to make an infusion, which was believed to allevi-

ate chest pains, while the Zuni claimed it cured snakebite. The Pawnee pulverized sunflower seeds with the roots of other plants to administer to pregnant women to fortify their milk. The sticky juice of the stem was prized for its curative power by the Cochiti, who utilized it to clean and dress wounds. The large leaves were often employed as bandages.

While archaeology and history link the sunflower to the northern regions of the Americas, European traditional lore cites Peru as the plant's original habitat. In his 1597 herbal, the British botanist John Gerarde claimed that sunflowers grew wild, "without sewing or setting, in Peru." The source of this belief has been the subject of much debate. The empires of the central and southern regions of the Americas, most notably that of the Aztecs, revered the sun as a source of power and life, and radiant disks figure prominently in their imagery. But the lack of archaeological evidence casts doubt as to whether sunflowers were first cultivated in the lands of the Aztec and the Inca, and the iconography of their imagery is significant for its solar, rather than its botanical, reference.

Sunflowers, along with maize, potatoes, tomatoes, and coco beans, were among the "new-world" plants shipped east across the Atlantic in the first

During his travels through the northeast territories of the Americas, the English artist John White made watercolor renderings of the villages he encountered. These first-hand images were often reused for other publications, enhanced with telling details. De Bry's engraving of Secota, an Algonquian settlement, is based on White's depiction of Secota, but De Bry added a circular garden plot and a stand of sunflowers in the lower-left corner of his reproduction of White's original image.

decades of the sixteenth century by Spanish expeditions. Peru was generally the last port of call for departing ships, and the early names developed by botanists to classify the sunflower, such as *Flos Solis peruvianus*, the "Marigolde of Peru," and the "Golden Flower of Peru," may have mistaken the country of the port of departure for a natural habitat. The tradition endured; as late as the nineteenth century, the German naturalist Alexander von Humboldt, who journeyed through South America between 1799 and 1804, declared with authority that "the *chimalatl* (Inca for marigold), or . . . the large flowers came from Peru to New Spain."

ABOVE LEFT John White, *The Indian Village of Secota*, c. 1570/80, black lead with watercolor on paper ABOVE RIGHT Theodore de Bry, *The Touun of Secota*, from *America*, 1590, engraving OPPOSITE Title page from John Parkinson, *Theatricum Botanicum*, 1640, woodcut

In the illustrated botanical *Theatricum Botanicum* (1640), John Parkinson defined the world as an abundant garden. The linked allegorical images in the title-page woodcut suggest this sphere of knowledge, presided over by Adam, caretaker of the first garden, and Solomon, the monarch of wisdom. Personifications of the four known continents—Asia, Africa, Europe, and America—feature the flora and fauna that distinguish these individual realms. America, seen in the lower right corner, holds aloft a bow and arrow. Dressed only in a skirt of feathers, she rides a llamalike creature through a landscape dotted with cactus, hedgehog thistle, and passion flowers. Looming above these exotic species are two giant sunflowers.

The Flower of Helios

Long before the sunflower journeyed east across the Atlantic Ocean, Europe had its own flowers of the sun. In the ancient Mediterranean world, naturalists studied the characteristics of flora and fauna. Texts such as the encyclopedic *Historia naturalis*, written in first-century Rome by Pliny the Elder, sought to clarify the mysteries of the physical universe, but in recording the particular attributes of plants and animals, naturalists also perpetuated traditional nature lore. One example was the phenomenon of heliotropic flowers, whose petal and leaf movements, turning from east to west or opening at dawn and closing at sunset, followed the sun's diurnal pattern. In their daily homage to solar rays, the so-called "heliotropes" came to be associated with the Greek myth of Clytie, a water nymph who perished for her love for Apollo, the Olympian deity of the sun.

Clytie adored Apollo and longed for him to return her ardor. Her hopes shattered when the god turned his attention to another, and Clytie descended into despair. For days she sat motionless, watching Apollo in his radiant chariot making his journey across the sky. Taking pity upon the love-struck nymph, Apollo changed her into a flower whose bright blossom con-

OPPOSITE Joachim von Sandrart, *Day*, 1643, oil on canvas ABOVE Causé (p. 23)

The solar association of the *Heliotropo magiore*, or "Greater Heliotrope," also known for its whiplash formation of petals into a "scorpion's tail," dates to the era of Imperial Rome. The long, flexible stalk of the heliotrope was twisted into a fillet to encircle the head of the emperor like a radiant crown. Its characteristic movement from east to west as the sun rises and sets inspired Christian theologians to regard it as a natural symbol of pious prayer. They urged Christians to turn toward their faith just as the heliotrope strained toward its source of light and life.

The *Calendula officinalis*, or common pot marigold, traces its European origins to the ancient Mediterranean region where it was prized for its medicinal powers. During the medieval era, a legend circulated that the Virgin Mary wore the bright, yellow-orange blossom on her breast as a symbol of the holy light that surrounded her. The little flower became known as "Mary's-bud" and "Mary's gold," and on Ladytide in England (March 25) churches were decorated with marigolds to honor the Annuciation. Its petals, said to open at dawn and close at dusk, inspired other names such as the Latin *solsequium* and the Old English *turn-sol*, both meaning "follow the sun."

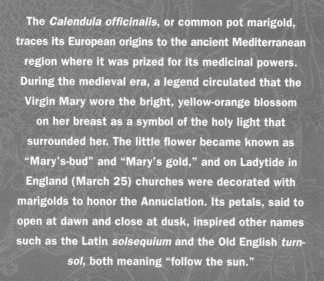

tinued to worship him, always turning its face to the sun. The sunflower or heliotrope became the emblem of submission to love, always constant, never questioning, and grateful for this emotion as a life force, even when the deepest devotion is not returned.

The Latin poet Ovid included the tale of Clytie and Apollo in his best-known work, *Metamorphoses*, written in the early years of the first century of the common era. His version of the myth, which includes Clytie's jealousy of Leucothoe, another nymph who found favor in Apollo's heart, endured through the Middle Ages and found a new, enthusiastic audience among the humanist scholars of the early Renaissance. This perpetuated a long-standing confusion of Apollo with Helios or the Roman Sol, the solar diety of the Olympian Pantheon. As the son of the Titian Hyperion, Helios was a generation older than Apollo. Every day he drove a golden chariot, drawn by four horses, across the sky from east to west, and his attribute was a golden disk with radiant beams, evoking his solar power. While Helios personified the course of the sun, Apollo embodied its warmth and its brightness. Over the centuries, Apollo usurped Helios's radiant agency, but Helios became the namesake for flowers that follow the sun's path.

By the seventeenth century, the floral lore associated with Helios and the new world sunflower fused. The cornucopia in this allegory of nature's fecundity holds European flowers, such as the lily and the rose, brought into bloom by the petal-strewn breath of the warm summer wind. Although new to European soil, the sunflower and the thistle also appear, springing naturally from the verdant ground of Apollo's grove.

OPPOSITE TOP From Gherado Cibo, *Heliotropo magiore*, 1565, colored engraving OPPOSITE BOTTOM *Of Marigolde*, from William Turner, *A New Herball*, 1551, woodcut ABOVE Henri Causé, *De Koninglycke Hovenier*, 1676, engraving

Over the course of the Middle Ages, two plants gained distinction as flowers of the sun. The first was the heliotrope. Although this is a general name given to those plants whose leaves and flowers turn toward the sun (helios meaning sun and trope signifying a turning), in the late Middle Ages the most common form in Europe featured closely clustered purple or white petals growing on a long, flexible stalk. Its whiplash form gave rise to the popular name of "Scorpion's tail." In the Roman era, the heliotrope was worn by the emperor, twined into a fillet to adorn his brow. Christian iconography adapted this use to encircle the halos of holy figures, including the Virgin Mary and the members of the Trinity. The characteristic movement of the heliotrope was seen as analogous to the pious soul, reaching in faith and fidelity toward the divine. To the fifth-century theologian

When Apollo rejected the affections of the water nymph Clytie, she descended into despair, refusing to eat, rest, or accept consolation. The French Baroque artist Charles de Lafosse depicted Clytie in the depths of her sorrow, weeping as her companions look on in helpless sympathy. The sunflower behind her echoes her desperate devotion; both flower and nymph strain toward the luminous but fleeting image of Apollo, as he drives his fiery chariot westward across the sky.

Charles de Lafosse, *The Nymph Clithea Transformed into Sunflowers*, 1688, oil on canvas

Proclus, the heliotrope symbolized prayer as it turns in praise to a greater power. In the sixteenth century, the British botanist William Turner linked the heliotrope with Greek mythology, stating: "Some thinke it to be *Herba Clytiae*, into which poets seigne *Clytia* to be metamorphosed."

The common marigold, which originated in the region of the Mediterranean and spread north and west to England, reigned as the other traditional European flower of the sun. Its concentric petals, ranging in tone from deep yellow to dark orange, suggest a sunburst. The belief that these petals opened at daybreak and closed at sunset strengthened this association and inspired the old English name *turn-sol*. Early in the development of Christian iconography, the marigold became an attribute of the Virgin Mary. According to legend, she wore a marigold on her breast as a symbol of the radiant light that sur-

In the late fourteenth century, the Gonzaga family, which ruled the Italian city-state of Mantua, adopted a stylized marigold as their device. It symbolized the fealty of son to father, as the power to govern Mantua passed from generation to generation. The recto of this medal features a portrait of Ludovico III, the second Marquess of Mantua, while the verso depicts him in armor, flanked by a marigold and a beaming sun. Through the image of the marigold paying homage to life-giving light, the medal declares Ludovico's filial devotion to the first Marquess, his father, Gianfrancesco.

rounded her. But in the seventeenth century, British poet Robert Herrick connected the flower with jealousy in the poem "How the Marigolds Came Yellow": "Jealous girls these sometimes were, / While they lived, or lasted here; / Turned to flowers, still they be / Yellow, marked for jealousy."

The marigold, with its radiant rings of petals and heliotropic movement, became an emblem of fealty to a greater power. The Gonzagas, who ruled Mantua during the Renaissance, chose it as their device in the late fourteenth century. A stylized marigold appears on medals honoring Gianfrancesco, the first Marquess, and his son Ludovico III. Ludovico's son Carlo also adopted the device, as well as the motto *Syn sus rayos meys desmayos* (Without his rays, I am nothing). In sixteenth-century France, Marguerite of Orléans, grandmother of King Henri IV, chose a marigold facing the sun for her coat of arms, explained by the motto *Je ne veux suivre que lui seul* (I will follow him only). But, as the new-world sunflower took root in European soil, it eclipsed the heliotrope and the marigold as the emblematic flower of the sun.

Antonio di Puccio Pisano (called Pisanello), *Medal Featuring Ludovico III Gonzaga, Second Marquess of Mantua* (TOP recto BOTTOM verso), 1447–48, bronze

To soothe Clytie's grief at his rejection of her, Apollo transformed the water nymph into a flower, but her devotion endured in the blossom's constant turning toward the sun. In Victorian England, as in previous centuries, artists depicted this moment of metamorphosis using the sunflower, which was unknown in the ancient Mediterranean world. The sorrowful features, straining neck, and twisting shoulders of George Frederick Watts's portrait bust of Clytie present her as the personification of eternal yearning, a woman trapped in a ring of radiating blossoms, a slave to her unrequited but unrelenting desire.

George Frederick Watts, *Clytie*, c. 1868, oil on panel

Deſcrib. a Dodon. f. 264.
Lobel. Obſ. 322.
Coeſalp. lib. 12. c. 35.
Lugdun. 874.
Nicol. Monard. Simpl. Medicam.
ex nouo orbe delatorü hiſtoriæ fol.
Hort. Med. Camer. 61.
Epit. Camer. 503.
Matth. C. Bauh. fol. 580.
Phyſtop. Caſp. Bauh. fol. 541.
Dalech. veſcalm ſpecimin
hiſt. plant. 291. 89.
Matth. Cam. 162.
Tabern. 430. lib. 2.
Durant. 766.

Botanical Profile

The sunflower that bloomed in the royal botanical garden in Madrid in 1510 is believed to be the first to be successfully cultivated in European soil. Along with the other plants—maize, tomatoes, peppers, chocolate, and potatoes—brought back from the Americas by Spanish explorers, the sunflower was prized as evidence of the continent's uncharted bounty. Yet, despite its diverse use in the west, Europeans dismissed the nutritional and medicinal potential of the tall, stately plant, growing it instead as a curiosity, a giant among domestic flowers with a spectacular and exotic appeal. Within a century, it was commonly cultivated in gardens across Europe. The rising popularity of the sunflower coincided with the evolution of European botanical science. As a wealth of information in the form of specimens and seedlings flowed into Europe, naturalists studied unknown flora. They recorded their observations, along with traditional knowledge and the lore carried back from the distant shores. These catalogues—known as herbals—named, described, and organized different plant types. Often handsomely illustrated, herbals laid the foundation for modern botanical taxonomy.

OPPOSITE Basilius Besler, *Flos Solismaior*, 1613, colored engraving ABOVE Crispijn de Passe the Younger, from Crispijn de Passe the Elder, *Hortis Floridus...*, 1614–17, engraving

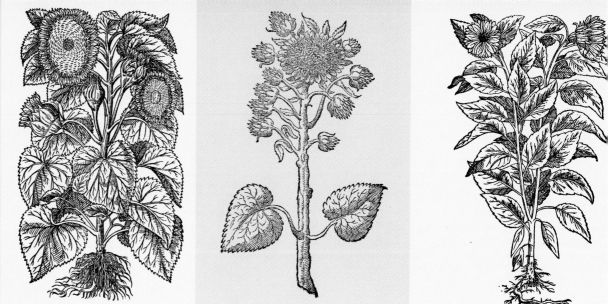

The first description of the sunflower appeared in Rembert Dodoens's *Florum, et Coronariarum...*, published in Antwerp in 1568. A new edition, with illustrations, was in demand by the following year. Dodoens's name for the flower, *Chrysanthemum perunianum*, likened its form to the domestic chrysanthemum and located its origins in Peru. Nicholas Monardes of Seville, in his *Joyfull Newes out of the Newe Founde Worlde* (English ed. 1577; original ed. 1574), merged the new-world sunflower with old-world heliotrope, claiming that "The Hearbe of the Sunne," with its flowers "greater then a greate Platter or Dishe," "doth tourne it-selfe continually towards the Sunne." The name "Marigolde of Peru," selected by naturalist John Gerarde in his *Herball or Generall Historie of Plantes* (1597), reveals his reliance upon an English translation of Dodoens's *Florum* by Henry Lyte (1578). Gerarde was impressed by the sunflower's extraordinary size and appearance, and, while

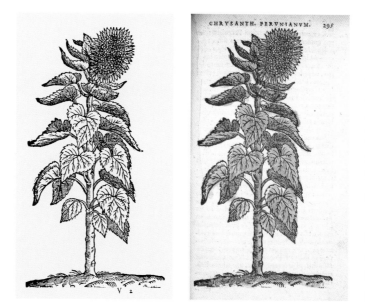

Rembert Dodoens's herbal, published in Antwerp in 1568, features the first European illustration of a sunflower. The woodcut, designed by Petrus van der Borcht, appears in subsequent editions and translations. In some editions, watercolor was applied by hand to enhance the black-and-white image.

noting that neither ancient nor modern writers assign a "virtue" (meaning utility) to the plant, he claimed that the "buddes . . . boiled and eaten with butter, vinegar, and pepper, are exceeding pleasant meate." In his herbal, *Paradisi in Sole: Paradisus Terretris* (1629), John Parkinson remarked that the dried heads of the "Golden Flower of Peru" were eaten much like "Hartichokes," but, he admitted, "They are too strong for my taste."

In the Netherlands, a new type of flower book developed along with the naturalist's herbal. The *florilegium* first appeared in the late sixteenth century. Consisting of a set of unbound sheets, engraved with botanical illustrations in black and white, the *florilegium* is essen-

John Miller, *Helianthus annus*, from *Illustratio Systematis Sexualis Linnaei*, 1777, colored engraving

ENGLISH **sunflower** FRENCH **tournesol or soleil** SPANISH **gira**
sol ITALIAN **girasole** DUTCH **zonnebloem** GERMAN **sor**
nenblume SWEDISH **solsikke** RUSSIAN **podsolnetschnik**

tially a picture book, published with little or no text. These images often surpass those in the herbals in their keen observation and meticulous rendering of botanical specimens, but the focus is on the blossom and foliage of the plant, with the roots and seeds rarely depicted. This suggests that the primary audience for *florilegia* were still-life painters looking for unusual flowers to include in a composition and artisans seeking patterns for decorations based on floral forms. Emanuel Sweerts, who sold bulbs and seeds as well as natural curiosities, conceived his *Florilegium* (1612) as a sales catalogue, to appeal to garden enthusiasts as well as artists. The subtitle of his work—*Indicis Plantis ad Vivum Delineatum*—states that living plants were used as models for the illustrations. Crispijn de Passe the Elder made a similar claim for his *Hortus Floridus* (1614–17), noting in his title that he had arranged the images himself and had them portrayed "with great effort from the life." While Sweerts sought new customers for his bulb trade, de Passe urged the owners

of his *florilegium* to color the black and white engravings for amusement.

The famed eighteenth-century Swedish naturalist Carolus Linnaeus gave the sunflower its enduring Latin name, *Helianthus annus*. At the time Linneaus developed his taxonomy, he

CLASS **Dicotyledones**
FAMILY **Compositae**
TRIBE **Helianthea**
GENUS **Helianthus**
SPECIES **Annuus**

believed that the sunflower was an annual plant, blooming only for a single season. To date nearly seventy types of sunflowers have been recognized, with more than a dozen annual species. The remaining types are perennials; most are cultivated as ornamental flowers, but the genus also includes the *Helianthus tuberosus*, known as the Jerusalem artichoke. All sunflowers are members of the *Compositae* family, along with marigolds, asters, dandelions, and daisies. The distinctive blossom consists of two parts: the dark, central disk made up of small, densely packed individual flowers; and the radiant petals. Each "disk flower" contains a complete reproductive system, with stamens, anthers, and pistils. The "ray flower"—composed of fused petals—is sterile and functions to attract bees to the disk. In writing about the *Helianthus annus*, Linneaus attributed his choice of name to his fascination with the sunflower's form: "And as one admires, presently the name occurs to the mind, even as, if one sees only the name, the admired picture of the flower comes before one."

ABOVE *Flos Solisminor mas, Flos Solisminor foemina*, from John Gerarde, *The Herbal or Generall Historie of Plantes*, 1597, colored woodcut
OPPOSITE Hans Simon Holtzbecker, *Sunflower*, from Gottorfer Codex, 1649–59, gouache on parchment

RAY FLOWERS

The petal-like arrangement along the outer rim of the flower head is made up of sterile, single ray flowers. Their sole function is to attract bees to pollinate the disk flowers.

BRACTS

Looking like sepals, they are actually phyllaries or little, greenish leaves at the back of the flower head.

FLOWER HEAD OR DISK

The central portion of the sunflower comprises hundreds of small, individual flowers packed together, called disk flowers.

ABOVE Frans Franken II and Workshop, *The Archdukes Albert and Isabella in a Collector's Cabinet*, c. 1626, oil on panel OPPOSITE TOP Crispijn de Passe the Elder, *A Decorative Garden in Summer*, from *Den Blom-Hof*, 1614, engraving OPPOSITE BOTTOM Title page from John Gerarde, *The Herball or Generall Historie of Plantes*, 1597, colored engraving

Interest in growing the sunflower slowly increased during the sixteenth century. By the early seventeenth century, it was regarded as a desirable and exotic cultivar for ornamental gardens. Featuring plants desirable for their scent and appearance, these geometrically planned gardens were a luxury. An impressive display demanded a considerable investment in unusual bulbs and seedlings, as well as a trained staff to keep the plots manicured and in bloom. Prized for their color and height, sunflowers were included as striking, single accents that towered over plants of a more modest scale. The interior counterpart to the ornamental garden was the collector's cabinet, a room devoted to precious and curious objects, ranging from fine paintings and decorative works to rare examples of natural wonders. In Franken's painting (left), the rulers of the Spanish Netherlands pay a visit to an ideal collector's cabinet. A sunflower is included among the unusual flora and fauna that appear alongside the inanimate treasures, crowning the spectacular bouquet positioned in the front left corner of the room.

To Follow the Sun

The flower garden, enjoyed solely for visual and aromatic pleasure, was long regarded as a luxury for the wealthy elite. But, during the late sixteenth and the seventeenth centuries, when the Netherlands gained prominence as the hub of commercial trade for Europe and its colonies throughout the world, this select circle of garden enthusiasts expanded to include members of the newly prosperous middle class. Merchants, bankers, speculators, and traders, these burgers had worked hard for their wealth, and they enjoyed the material status it brought them. They decorated their homes with handsome and expensive appointments and wore garments made of sumptuous fabrics and furs. A flower garden often figured in this prosperous display. Although small in scale when compared to the grand gardens of royalty after which they were modeled, the gardens of the affluent middle class featured distinctive blooms. The English nurseryman John Rae commented that an ideal garden should take "the form of a Cabinet, with several Boxes fit to receive, and securely keep, Natures' choicest jewels." While the sunflower never enjoyed the outrageous popularity of the tulip in the Netherlands, which led to a speculative economic crisis known as Tulipomania (1634–37), Crispijn de Passe the

OPPOSITE From *Amoris Divini Emblemata. Studio et Aere Othonis Vaeni Concinnata*, 1615, woodcut

ABOVE *Vultu Non Exatian Tur Amato*, from Julius Wilhelm Zincgreff, *Emblematum Ethico-politcorum Centuria IVLII*, 1619, woodcut

Elder placed it among "the rarest and excellentest flowers" in his *Hortus Floridus,* and the sunflower became a favorite element in these new gardens.

While the pleasure of a floral garden was seasonal, flowers depicted in art could lend brightness and beauty to a home throughout the year. The demand for floral still-life paintings in the lowlands rose in tandem with the cultivation of personal gardens, and sunflowers became a stable feature of painted bouquets. Gerard de Lairesse, author of *Groot Schilderboek* (1707), a manual for flower painters, urged artists to combine flowers with sensitivity to "kracht en uitwerking" (proper force and effect) in order to enliven the composition with contrasts of size and color. For example a large yellow sunflower, surrounded by many small blossoms in tones of purple, violet, and blue, made a pleasing bouquet. Lairesse also assigned meaning to colors, stating that yellow indicated pomp or glory. It was his belief that "if one but places the emblematic flower in the middle, that is enough: the rest one can fill with such colors as one finds satisfactory, so long as they advance somewhat less toward the eye." He also provided rules for painting floral decoration on walls and ceilings, noting that large, colorful flowers, such as the sunflower, should be positioned in the center or at the ends of garlands and swags to anchor such elements.

Some painters turned to the older iconography of the heliotrope and the marigold when including sunflowers in

Both bright and bold, the sunflower was regarded as a natural decorative element in seventeenth-century floral still lifes. While painters favored the sunflower for its vivid color and distinctive shape, they used it sparingly; they found that just one or two blossoms in a composition anchored the arrangement or provided a contrast to more subtle tones.

LEFT, TOP TO BOTTOM. Bosschaert (see below); Jean Baptiste Monnoyer, *Sunflowers, Foxgloves, Honeysuckle and Other Flowers in an Urn on a Ledge* (detail), late seventeenth century, oil on canvas; de Heem (page 8); van Walscapelle (page 39)
RIGHT Ambrosius Bosschaert the Younger, *Vase of Flowers with a Monkey,* c. 1630/45, oil

ABOVE Jakob van Walscapelle, *Vase of Flowers on a Marble Base*, 1672, oil on canvas

their displays. The sunflower crowning Ambrosius Bosschaert the Younger's *Vase of Flowers with a Monkey* indicates the constancy of faith, in harmony with such traditional symbols as grapes (wine of the Eucharist), a pomegranate (death and ressurection), and a tethered monkey (controlling animal instincts). Sunflowers also featured in genre paintings, such as Frans van Mieris the Elder's *A Boy Blowing Bubbles* (1663). Here, the sunflower amplifies the modest moral message: the bursting bubble represents the transitory nature of pleasure, while the vital sunflower, in its constant submission to a higher power, demonstrates the enduring rewards of faith. Following the traditional tale of Clytie, the sunflower also became a sign for the ardent lover. In *Amorum Emblemata* (1608), Otto van Veen paired the image of Cupid pointing to the radiant sun, and a sunflower in an elegant garden straining up toward warmth and light with the text "As the flowre heliotrope doth to the Sunnes cours bend, / Right so the lover doth unto his love enclyne." As an emblem, Cupid and the sunflower generally proclaimed a dual meaning: profane love for a mortal being is but a shadow of sacred love, which is ever directed toward the divine. But among the burghers of the Netherlands, the sunflower also served to celebrate marital fidelity—embodying both the devotion of a good spouse and the hierarchy of a marriage in which the wife follows her husband—and it

Jan Weenix, *Hunting Still Life with Hound and Monkey before a Garden*, 1687, oil on canvas

Frans van Mieris the Elder, *A Boy Blowing Bubbles*, 1663, oil on panel

"I still adore my sire with prostrate face,
Turn where he turns, and all his motions trace."

ABRAHAM CROWLEY, "Sun-Flower," *History of Plants*, c. 1640

The sunflower always turns
in pursuit of the sun.
So too does a lover,
who turns to his love,
There he sends his heart
and soul and face
To see her always as his
greatest longing.

OTTO VAN VEEN
Amorum Emblemata, 1608

The emblem of Cupid observing the sunflower's constant
homage to the sun appeared early in the seventeenth
century. Its meaning was two-fold: profane love for an
earthly companion and sacred love for the divine.

became a common feature in portraits of engaged couples.

In England heliotropic flowers signified the obedience of a subject to his liege, as well as his dependence upon his patron for favor. William Shakespeare's twenty-fifth sonnet declares: "Great Princes' favorites their fair leaves spread, / But as the Marigold at the Sun's eye, / And in themselves their pride lies buried, / For at a frown they in their glory die." The Flemish painter Anthony van Dyke may have employed the sunflower in a self-por-

trait of 1633 as a signal of loyalty to England, his adopted country. He had received that very year from his patron Charles I the gold chain he wears in the portrait. With his left hand, van Dyke fingers the chain, while in his right, he holds a massive sunflower, recalling the words of Francis Thynne in his *Emblems and Epigrams Presented to Sir Thomas Egerton* (1600): "Just as the sunflower turns to the sun for strength and sustenance, so the subject turns toward his monarch." But the sunflower may also represent van Dyke's

profession. In his native land, it was also used to express an artist's obedience to nature, drawing inspiration from its beauty in the same way the sunflower draws strength from the sun. In 1654 Joost van den Vondel celebrated the art of painting in a poem written for the feast of Saint Luke, the patron saint of painters. "Just as the sunflower turns its eyes in love toward the vault of heaven . . . so the Art of Painting, from inborn inclination, kindled by a sacred fire, follows the beauty of nature."

OPPOSITE LEFT Boëtius Bolswert, *Ego dilecto meo*, from Herman Hugo, *Pia Desideria*, 1624, engraving OPPOSITE RIGHT From Otto van Veen, *Amorum Emblemata*, 1608, engraving
ABOVE Jan Steen, *Peasants before an Inn*, early 1650s, oil on panel

"Just as the sunflower turns its eyes in love
toward the vault of heaven . . . so the Art of Painting
. . . follows the beauty of nature."

JOOST VAN DEN VONDEL, "Inauguration of the Art of
Painting on Saint Luke's Feast," 1654

The sunflower in Antony van Dyke's *Self-Portrait* holds a triple meaning. Born in Flanders, the painter may have wanted to invoke the traditional meaning of the flower as a sign of Christian piety. But, working in England, he may have also employed the sunflower as an attribute to declare his loyalty to his patron King Charles I, as well as his fidelity as an artist to the supreme model of nature

The iconography of this portrait of an unidentified young woman praises her potential as a faithful wife. The pearls she wears signifies her purity, while the vase of roses suggest her capacity to love. The rock supporting the vase announces that she will be steadfast. In this context, the sunflower celebrates marital fidelity; she will be as unceasing in her devotion to her husband as the flower is to its namesake. This iconography extends to Ferdinand Bol's depiction of a handsome, young couple, whose commitment to constancy is signaled by the sunflower at the lower right.

OPPOSITE Antony van Dyke, *Self-Portrait with Sunflower*, 1633, oil on canvas ABOVE LEFT Ferdinand Bol, *Portrait of a Couple*, 1654, oil on canvas ABOVE RIGHT Karel de Moor, *Woman with Roses and Sunflowers*, late 17th/early 18th century, oil on panel

Radiant Spirit

Throughout the history of Christian thought, the image of the Garden of Eden has presented a metaphor of the power and breadth of divine bounty. As the European world view widened, the image of the natural wealth of paradise diversified. The frontispiece to John Parkinson's herbal *Paradisi in Sole, Paradisus Terrestris* (1627) portrays Adam and Eve in a verdant forest where exotic plants—cactus, pineapple, palm trees, and tulips—grow among trees and flowers native to Europe. Parkinson's vision of paradise also includes a sunflower. By the early seventeenth century, the sunflower had acquired a specific Christian significance. Its heliotropic movement was seen as an analogue for the pious soul. When paired with the image of Adam and Eve, the devoted sunflower countered their transgression, demonstrating how to resist any and all temptation. Within the century, the sunflower joined the symbols of the lily and the rose as attributes of the Madonna. The lily embodied her purity and the rose her having been chosen above all other women, but the sunflower represented her human soul, turning like its namesake to the life-giving light by following the teachings of Christ.

OPPOSITE Antonio Ponce, *The Ascension of the Virgin*, 1654, oil on canvas ABOVE *Christi, actio imitatio nostra*, from Zacharias Heyns, *Emblemata, Sinne-Beelden*, 1625, woodcut

PARADISI IN SOLE
Paradisus Terrestris.
or
A Garden of all sorts of pleasant flowers which our
English ayre will permitt to be noursed vp:
with
A Kitchen garden of all manner of herbes, rootes, & fruites,
for meate or sause vsed with vs,
and
An Orchard of all sorte of fruitbearing Trees
and shrubbes fit for our Land
together
With the right orderings planting & preseruing
of them and their vses & vertues
Collected by John Parkinson
Apothecary of London
1629

While botanical books of the seventeenth century portray indigenous plants of the western hemisphere as nature's marvels, contemporary emblem books—a kind of iconographic catalogue—present the new-world wonders as part of the rich diversity of divine bounty. The title page of John Parkinson's 1627 *Paradisi in Sole Paradisus Terrestris* characterizes the natural world as an earthly paradise, a Garden of Eden flourishing under a benevolent sun. In an era that sought symbolic significance in all forms of art, the scientific act of naming was intertwined with the spiritual habit of instilling meaning in representation; newly discovered flora, such as the cactus, tulip, and sunflower, gained significance in concert with conventional symbols such as the lily, ivy, and apple tree.

Exotic plants and animals peacefully coexist with domestic breeds in Roelant Savery's vision of Paradise. Most likely the artist never actually saw such strange and beautiful creatures as the camel, but he rendered them according to vivid descriptions. One can just make out, deep in the background at the left of the composition, the tiny figures of Adam and Eve near an apple tree. In the foreground at the far right, sunflowers nod on sturdy stalks. By the early seventeenth century, the sunflower had acquired the heliotropic reference of pious devotion. Shown blooming in Eden, it was intended to demonstrate obedience to divine will, in contrast to humanity's lax resistance to temptation.

In the course of the seventeenth century, the sunflower served to illustrate many forms of devotion and constancy, that of a subject to a patron, a wife to a husband, a child to a parent, or a lover to his or her beloved. But the concurrent rise of emblem books established the piety of a Christian soul as the sunflower's dominant meaning in European culture. Emblem books feature a set of woodcuts or engravings paired with mottos, epi-

grams, or a brief verse. The text gives meaning to the individual image, transforming it into a "speaking picture" that then conveys its message without verbal explanation.

The earliest emblem books, which appeared well before the middle of the sixteenth century, have a secular focus, but by the end of the century, these iconographic catalogues were used to promote personal religious devotion. While Nicolai Revsneri's *Emblemata,*

published in Frankfurt in 1581, urges his readers to follow the example of Christ, just as Clytie followed the light of Apollo, it neither mentions nor illustrates a sunflower. But by the first quarter of the seventeenth century, the sunflower turning in homage to a radiant sun was well established as an emblem. In Zacharias Heyns's *Emblemata, Sinne-Beelden,* published in 1625, a robust sunflower straining toward a beaming sun appears under

OPPOSITE Title page from John Parkinson, *Paradisi in Sole, Paradisus Terrestris*, 1627, woodcut ABOVE Roelant Savery, *Paradise, with The Fall*, 1628, oil on copper

the motto "Christi, actio imitatio nostra" (Christ's action is our model). Below the image are the words of Christ to the scribes and Pharisees as recorded in John 8:12: "I am the light of the world: he who follows me shall not walk in darkness, but shall have the light of life."

Emblem books transcended religious difference. *Heliotropium: Seu Conformation Humnea Vuluntatis cum Divina* (1627), by Jeremias Drexelius, a Jesuit priest and a professor of humanities at the University of Augsberg, went through many editions and was circulated widely

among Catholic and Protestant readers alike. In his *Proteus ofte Minnebeelden* (1627), Dutch poet and statesman Jacob Catz combined his classical learning with Calvinist morals to produce a lexicon of mundane images to promote pious behavior among the citizens of an increasingly secular society. No

Francesco Solimena (attrib.), *Rest on the Flight into Egypt*, 1695, oil on copper

Jeremias Drexelius wrote and published the emblem book *The Heliotropium* in 1627. Very popular in the seventeenth century among both Catholic and Protestant readers, it enjoyed a revival in the nineteenth century, when it was translated into several languages, including English. In urging the reader to follow Christ's example, each image shown here presents a sunflower as an emblem of constancy.

ABOVE From Jeremias Drexelius, *The Heliotropium, or Conformity of the Human Will to the Divine*, 1863 (first edition, 1627)

A Sun-flower the sun shining upon it. *Vota sequntur*. My desire is after you.

A Sun-flower. *Solem sola sequor*. I follow the sun.

The Nymph *Clitye* lying and languishing upon the Earth, and, behind her, a Marygold inclining towards the Sun. *Sic dignus Amari*. I merit Love.

A Sun-flower drooping. *Sino che torni*. Till the Sun returns.

matter the intended audience, the sunflower assumed iconic significance as the eternal example of the devout soul, ever grateful for the light of the divine.

The language of emblems endured into the eighteenth century, often reworked for young readers. The anonymous *Emblems for the Entertainment and Improvement of Youth*, published around 1729, features several images of sunflowers paired with mottos, including a thriving plant illustrating "My desire is after you" and a languishing blossom that will droop "Till the sun returns." In the nineteenth century, in German art and culture, sunflowers express the vitality of youth, as seen in Philipp Otto Runge's portrait *The Hülsenbeck Children* (1805). The education reformer Friedrich Froebel envisioned the realm of early learning as a "kindergarten," an ideal and natural paradise, and in the fanciful illustrations of his *Mutter-und Koselieder* (Mother's Songs, Games, and Stories) of 1844, broad disks of giant sunflowers provide sturdy playgrounds for innocent children.

The spiritual dimension of the sunflower's iconography also proved a potent symbol for the pantheism of German Romantic thought. By regarding divine power as a transcendent

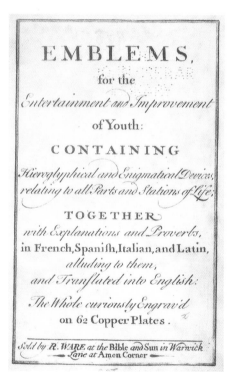

Emblem books reached the zenith of their influence in the seventeenth century, but the tradition endured, most notably in editions directed a young audience as instruction for moral behavior.

force, a mystery that eludes human comprehension, pantheism sought the manifestation of God in nature and defined the natural world as material proof of divine intention. In *Confessions from the Heart of an Art Loving Monk* (1797), a treatise intended to inspire piety in artistic endeavors, Wilhelm Wackenroder described how his thoughts often turned to his favorite works of art "spontaneously, like the sunflower to the sun." He urged artists to create in a spirit that was mindful of divine intention, in the manner that "God looks on all of Nature." Subtle, but ever-present, sunflowers appear in Romantic paintings of nature, symbolizing a model of gratitude toward divine creation. More than a generation later, Vincent van Gogh would echo this desire to freely submit to divine will, writing to his brother Theo from Amsterdam in April 1878: "*Le rayon d'en haut* [The light from above] does not always shine upon us and may well be hidden behind clouds, but without that light a man cannot live and is worth nothing and can do no good."

TOP, LEFT TO RIGHT, From *Emblems. . .* (see below), engravings BOTTOM Title page from *Emblems for the Entertainment and Improvement of Youth. . .*, 1729

52

The stand of sunflowers that thrusts skyward
above the youngest of the three Hülsenbeck children gives
form to the vital spirit that pervades this 1805
portrait. Like the sunflowers, the children seem to embody
organic energy drawn from the warmth of the sun.

Friedrich Froebel, a pioneer in early education, created a
series of simple songs for his program that could be
paired with activities such as dancing and gardening.
The illustrations in this collection depict the *kindergarten*
as an imaginative realm where children play on the
gigantic blossom of a sunflower.

ABOVE Philipp Otto Runge, *The Hülsenbeck Children*, 1805, oil on canvas BOTTOM RIGHT *Däumcher neig' dich...*, from Friedrich Froebel, *Mutter-und Koselieder*, 1844

Pantheism informed the spiritual ideal of German Romanticism. In the belief that the mysteries of the universe are beyond human comprehension, Romantic thinkers looked to the natural world for material evidence of the transcendent divine. As one of the glories of nature, the sunflower provided an apt icon for belief in its unquestioning and constant homage to the source of all life. Sunflowers often appear in imagery of churchyards and cemeteries, growing untended as proof that the divine spirit is continually manifest in nature.

OPPOSITE Karl Friedrich Schinkel, *Gothic Church Behind a Tree*, 1810, lithograph with white heightening
ABOVE Sophie Reinhard, *By the Grave*, from *Poems in the Dialect of the Upper Rhine Region*, 1820, etching

> "I am the light of the world: he who follows me shall not walk in darkness, but shall have the light of life."
>
> *John* 8:12

In his illustrations for an edition of the *New Testament*, the English artist James Tissot depicted the human dimension of Christ's nature. The frontispiece, inspired by lines from the *Song of Solomon* in the Old Testament, portrays Christ as a patient, concerned, yet ever-vigilant presence: "Behold, he standeth behind our wall, he looketh forth at the shadows showing himself through the lattice." The kind face of Christ can be seen watching from behind the lattice in Tissot's design. Ripe, glossy grapes hang from a vine twining around the lattice, recalling Christ's sacrifice as embodied in the Eucharist. Sunflower stalks lift their broad blossoms as if to surround the openings in the wall, instructing the pious to do the same in devoting themselves to Christ.

James Tissot, *Jesus Looking through a Lattice with Sunflowers*, frontispiece for New Testament, 1886–94, gouache

Summer's Glory

The sunflower quickly lost its status as an exotic bloom as it spread throughout the gardens of Europe. Its ungainly height and coarse stalk now seemed crude next to more delicate flowering plants; thus, in the early nineteenth century, sunflowers were confined to the back walls and corners of gardens. They were seen as too rustic for elegant plots. As an anonymous writer in *Ladies' Horticulture* noted, despite the majesty of its size, the sunflower was "very often excluded from the parterre, which admits many others far inferior in splendour and dignity." Hardy and requiring little attention, the sunflower was easily cultivated. The same author instructed her readers to find a corner of the courtyard "where the paving is displaced . . . [and] drop a [sunflower] seed there in April." Nature itself would bring the seedling into bloom. In an era of floral culture, when botanical studies, gardening, and flower arranging were regarded as suitable and even desirable activities for women, cultivating sunflowers provided little challenge and brought little admiration. In fact William Makepiece Thackeray alluded to female vulgarity through the image of the bold, yellow bloom. In his novel *Vanity Fair* (1848),

OPPOSITE Claude Monet, *Bouquet of Sunflowers*, 1881, oil on canvas ABOVE Eugène Delacroix (p. 61)

he characterized the modest charms of his heroine Amelia Sedley with the following comment: "There are garden ornaments as big as brass-warming pans, that are fit to stare the sun itself out of countenance. Miss Sedley was not of the sunflower sort."

Yet in the previous century, in a four-book poem "The Seasons" (1726–30), James Thompson envisioned the sunflower as a natural feature in a pastoral idyll. "Summer," written in 1727, traces the course of a halcyon day, during which shepherds shear their sheep and harvest hay in concert with the cycle of the rising and setting sun. For Thompson "the lofty follower of the sun" symbolized the glory of summer, when solar rays warm the earth to regenerate fallow nature. The hardy vigor that made the sunflower too crude for an elegant garden came to embody a rustic ideal. By the mid-nineteenth century, as industry and urban congestion increased in both Europe and the United States, the sunflower began to symbolize healthy, wholesome, and simple agrarian existence. Naturalist painters captured a vital life force in portraying the flower's strong form and vibrant tone. Whether cultivated near a garden shed or cottage door or featured in a rustic bouquet, the sunflower signified a new passion for the pastoral as an alternative to the complexities of modern life.

For the French painter Claude Monet, the sunflower expressed the joyous vitality of summer. He was an avid gardener, and whenever possible

ABOVE Johan Christian Dahl, *Julie Vogel in Her Garden near Dresden*, 1825/28, oil on canvas

But one, the lofty follower of the sun
Sad when he sets, shuts up her yellow leaves,
Drooping all night, and when he warm returns
Points her enamour'd bosom to his ray.

JAMES THOMSON, "Summer,"
The Seasons, 1727

LEFT Eugène Delacroix, *Sunflowers*, from a sketch book, 1855–59, graphite on paper RIGHT Michael Ancher, *Girl with Sunflowers*, 1889, oil on canvas
BACKGROUND Pietro Andrea Mattioli (p. 30)

he chose to live in the suburbs of Paris, where he could tend his own flower beds. In the autumn of 1878, he rented a house in Vétheuil, a quiet village sixty kilometers north of Paris. A steep flight of stairs led from the road to his house, and Monet flanked them with sunflowers. During his last summer in Vétheuil, he painted his youngest son Michel and Jean Pierre Hoschedé, the youngest son of his companion, Alice, standing between the lofty rows. Two years later, in 1883, Monet moved to Giverny, and sunflowers were among the first plants he cultivated in his new garden. Over the years, the flower garden grew to spectacular proportions; while his water garden became most famous, the sunflower remained, with irises and lilies, among his favorites. Monet preferred the common annual, collecting seeds each autumn for the following summer's garden, and he also imported varieties of perennials from England. With careful planting, the artist enjoyed sunflowers from the first days of warmth in June through the waning of the season in September. As late as 1920, despite his failing eyesight, Monet introduced new varieties of sunflowers into his garden, and when he had no more room for them along the house and walkway borders, he had them planted between the trees in his orchard.

The cultivation of sunflowers spread east from Europe through the Balkans and into Russia. When Peter the Great of Russia toured Europe in 1697, he col-

ABOVE Jan Toorop, *Seduction*, 1886, oil on canvas OPPOSITE Claude Monet, *The Artist's Garden at Vétheuil*, 1881, oil on canvas

62

lected sunflower seeds as a curiosity, which he had planted when he returned home. By the nineteenth century, Russia boasted vast fields of the vigorous plant. While Europe had little use for the sunflower as a food crop, in Russia the sunflower seed became a popular source for oil, particularly during the Orthodox Lent, when conventional high-fat foods were banned by the church. In the 1870s, groups of Mennonite immigrants brought Russian varieties to the southern prairie lands of Manitoba. Shortly afterward, a distinctive, giant sunflower—known as the Mammoth Russian—appeared in American seed catalogues, completing over the course of the centuries the sunflower's circuit of the globe.

In the gentle light of a warm afternoon, the young girl in Jacob Maris's painting trims a straw hat with wildflowers. The sunflowers— one turning toward the child and the other toward the church in the distance—add a dimension of reverence to her simple task.

OPPOSITE Jessica Hallyar, *Autumn Sunlight*, 1891, watercolor ABOVE Jacob Maris, *A Girl Seated outside a House*, 1867, oil on mahogany

In nineteenth-century United States, the sunflower was regarded as a humble plant, hardy and bright but too coarse and common for the cultivated garden. According to popular lore in the rural communities of the southern states, a dream of sunflowers forecasted wounded pride, which could be reversed by picking a perfect bloom before the next night's sleep. Texans are known to have believed that a wish made on a sunflower plucked before dusk was certain to come true. In this painting of a country lad in ragged clothes, the sunflower perhaps expresses innocent youth, as natural yet as ephemeral as the butterfly perched on the child's shoulder. But the painting also presents one of the major achievements of the Civil War, giving African-Americans the right to attend school.

Winslow Homer, *Taking a Sunflower to Teacher*, 1875, oil on canvas

The common sunflower, native to the plains states, was regarded as little more than a weed in early nineteenth-century America. Grown for fodder rather than food, the flower inspired an anonymous couplet that laments its lack of refinement: "The sunflower 'tis rank and coarse / 'Twould make a lovely bouquet for a horse." During the Civil War, poor southern households roasted its seeds to make a substitute for coffee. In Texas the stems and flowers were burned to make potash to stoke baking ovens, and local lore claimed that a wish made upon a sunflower plucked before sunset was guaranteed to be fulfilled. In 1903 the state of Kansas chose the sunflower as its floral emblem. Defined in the Session Laws proclamation as a wildflower that grew throughout the state, the sunflower was hailed as hardy and praised for its striking appearance, "with its strong, distinct disk and its golden circle of . . . glowing rays." Although Kansas became "The Sunflower State," by the turn of the twentieth century, thousands of acres of sunflowers bloomed across the American heartland, becoming for the midwestern and plains states a staple crop and one of the most welcome sights of summer.

This flower has to all Kansans a historic symbolism which speaks of frontier days, winding trails, pathless prairies, and is full of life and glory of the past, the pride of the present, and richly emblematic of the majesty of a golden future, and is a flower which has given Kansas the worldwide name, "The Sunflower State."

Session Laws of Kansas, 1903

George Dunlop Leslie, *Sun and Moonflowers*, 1889, oil on canvas

Sun and Style

As a student at Oxford University, William Morris wrote "The Story of the Unknown Church" (1856), a prose romance set in the Middle Ages. His narrator is a fictional, twelfth-century stone mason, who recalls the beauty of a church cloister bordered by "many sunflowers that were all in blossom on that autumn day." Morris had visited the ruins of medieval churches and had studied illuminated manuscripts in the Bodleian Library, and, although the sunflower did not appear in any of his authentic sources, he imagined that it could grow in that long-lost cloister. Morris, who went on to found and lead the Arts and Crafts Movement, was not alone in revising the sunflower's botanical history. The majestic flower appears in many of the poems and paintings of Victorian Britain that idealize the Middle Ages. Robert Browning made it the emblem of a Provençal troubadour in his poem "Rudel to the Lady of Tripoli" (1842), while Morris's friend the painter Edward Burne-Jones drew the young knight of "Childe Roland," inspired by another poem by Browning (1855), standing in a field of sunflowers (1861). These imaginative inventions, prompted by the sunflower's strong, heraldic form, marked the first step in the transformation of the flower's role in nineteenth-century artistic

OPPOSITE Kate Hayllar, *Sunflowers and Hollyhocks* (detail), 1889, oil on canvas ABOVE Jeckyll (p. 74)

William Morris included sunflowers in many of his early decorative designs, recognizing a natural heraldic aesthetic in the dark disk surrounded by radiant petals. In 1861 William Morris and his like-minded friends formed a corporation to promote higher standards in the decorative arts through fine craftsmanship and hand-finished production. William de Morgan was among the many artists who provided designs for "The Firm." His tiles and his lusterware vessels drew inspiration from nature as well as tradition, two of the touchstones of Morris's Arts and Crafts philosophy.

LEFT William Morris (designer), *Autumn*, c.1873, stained glass RIGHT William de Morgan (designer), *Sunflower Tiles*, 1880s, glazed earthenware BACKGROUND Morris (p. 74)

circles, a fantastic journey from the humble corner of the country garden to a place of honor in the most fashionable drawing rooms of England and North America.

The ornamental form of the sunflower appealed to Burne-Jones, who described it as "a whole school of drawing and an education in itself." But the painter also cast it as a whimsical character, sometimes brazen and proud, sometimes shy, and often wearing "bees for brooches in most admirable taste." He claimed that "it is so right to make [sunflowers] talk mottos; they all look as if they were thinking," and he was enchanted with epigrams in emblem books, such as *absente sole languesco* (when the sun is absent I languish) and *usque ad reditum* (it followed not inferior things), declaring, "Bless them, they say lovely things" when they gaze upon the sun. Morris also was intrigued by the decorative shape of the sunflower. He openly disliked showy hybrids, dismissing the double sunflower as "coarse-coloured and dull." He preferred the common variety, which grew in abundance in the gardens surrounding the Red House, his home in Upton. From his studio windows, Morris could view his gardens, and the natural forms of the flowers inspired his wallpaper and textile designs.

Morris's credo "Have nothing in your houses which you do not know to be useful or believe to be

Edward Burne-Jones, *Scenes from the Life of Saint Frideswide*, 1859 and c. 1890, oil on paper

"Have nothing in your houses which you do not know to be useful or believe to be beautiful."

WILLIAM MORRIS, "The Beauty of Life," 1880

Charles Ashbee (designer), *Piano Cover* (detail), c. 1889, gold thread and appliqué on silk damask

beautiful" was a founding principle for the Arts and Crafts Movement. The homes he decorated featured traditionally crafted furniture and hand-painted art tiles, as well as papers and textiles with decorative floral patterns. Morris's clients, affluent, upper-middle class art collectors, embraced the new style as a signature of advanced taste throughout Great Britain, and Morris's ideas influenced other designers, such as the ceramic artist William de Morgan and architects Charles Ashbee and Thomas Jeckyll. Through travel, imported goods, and illustrated design journals, the Arts and Crafts ideal rapidly crossed the Atlantic, and the American response ranged from the fine, carved furniture of the Herter Brothers of New York to the natural ornament on the vases made by Rookwood Pottery in Cincinnati. Morris used the strong, basic form of the sunflower for a wallpaper pattern in 1877. By that time, it had become a popular ornament in Arts and Crafts design in a wide array of materials, carved or inlaid to decorate wooden furniture, cast in iron as railings and firedogs, and worked in textiles as curtains, rugs, and hangings.

Architects, including Richard Norman Shaw and W. Eden Nesfield, also responded to the Arts and Crafts aesthetic, developing a picturesque domestic style called "Queen Anne." In the 1870s and 1880s, "Queen Anne" mansion flats and town homes were built in Chelsea, Kensington, and Bedford Park. These fashionable

H. W. Batley used sunflowers as ornamental accents in this carved, boxwood panel he designed for a piano made in London by James Shoolbred and Company in 1878.

The sunflower was a favorite motif of Arts and Crafts designers. Whether carved in wood or cast in iron, its singular shape had a distinctive ornamental appeal that could stand alone or be repeated as a natural element in a decorative pattern.

LEFT Thomas Jeckyll (designer), *Sunflower Ornament*, 1876, wrought iron
TOP RIGHT Probably Lewis F. Day (designer), *Clock*, 1880, ebonized wood, porcelain, and glass ABOVE William Morris, *Design for "Sunflower" Wallpaper*, 1879, graphite on paper

London districts were associated with artists and art patrons who supported Arts and Crafts ideals, and the cast terracotta panels that decorated the exteriors of their new red-brick homes became a standard feature of contemporary art and design, with sunflowers as the favorite motif.

While Morris stressed the alliance of beauty and utility, another movement in British design advocated the cultivation of beauty in the home for its own sake. Like the Arts and Crafts Movement, the Aesthetic Movement endeavored to raise the standards of domestic interior design and provide a quality alternative to cheap manufactured goods. But devotees of the Aesthetic Movement valued rarity over practicality as they attempted to live their lives in state of elevated artistic

The Aesthetic Movement encouraged women to express their artistic sensibility through dress and interior design. In contrast to prevailing fashions, female aesthetes abandoned confining tight bodices and unwieldy bustles for loose garments that followed the body's natural lines. With her husband, Percy, Madeline Wyndham collected contemporary art and regularly held dinners for artists in her elegant London home. Her distinctive gown of dark-green velvet, ornamented with embroidered sunflowers is an example of "artistic dress," a mode that Henry James described as timeless, "simple yet splendid."

George Frederick Watts, *Study for Portrait of Mrs. Percy Wyndham*, c. 1877, oil on canvas

Aesthetic Movement interiors featured Japanese prints and such motifs as sunflowers, peacock feathers, and lilies as ornamental embellishments. All were prized for their inherent beauty, rather than their cultural significance or traditional iconography. The sunflower became so pervasive in Aesthetic Movement design that it served as an emblem of advanced taste.

TOP LEFT Kawamura Kihō, *Sunflower*, 1824, color woodblock print BOTTOM LEFT Rookwood Pottery (Agnes Pittman, decorator), *Sunflower Vase*, 1885, glazed and gilded earthenware RIGHT Lawrence Alma-Tadema, *Sunflowers*, last quarter nineteenth century, oil on canvas

sensibility. The elements of the Aesthetic Movement interior were eclectic, mixing medieval furniture and antique textiles with Japanese prints and screens, painted fans, and blue-and-white porcelain ware imported from Asia. Women adopted a mode of "artistic dress," disdaining the conventional corset, bustle, and crinoline in favor of loose, unstructured garments made of mat silks and velvets, muted in tone and often embroidered with flowers. Lilies, peacock feathers, and sunflowers functioned as decorative forms in every aspect of domestic decor or were displayed as objects of inherent beauty. As a self-declared style of the elite, the Aesthetic Movement soon attracted the barbs of the popular press. In 1882 the humor journal *Punch* parodied female aesthetes "who *sigh* for SUNFLOWERS . . . and peruse improper POEMS." The fashion for aestheticism was brief, rising in the late 1870s and waning in the early 1880s, but it gave the sunflower a new and lasting identity as a sign of high aesthetic taste.

American Arts and Crafts designers also favored the sunflower as a decorative motif. New York furniture makers the Herter Brothers employed carved sunflowers to embellish the cabinet portion of this imposing piece.

Herter Brothers, *Sideboard*, 1876–80, oak with white pine

Walter Crane's fondness for sunflowers influenced his designs. He repeated them as ornaments in his frieze patterns for tile decoration and murals, but he also liked to portray them as whimsical characters for children's books, such as this personification of "August," dressed as a sailor with a sunburnt face. In 1897 he hosted a fancy-dress ball and designed a sunflower costume for his wife to wear.

The mid-nineteenth century saw the emergence of a new type of book for children, the illustrated "toybook." In her contributions to this genre, Kate Greenaway often included sunflowers in settings for her charming images, adding a bright and cheerful element to the design. An accomplished botanical artist, Greenaway also made carefully observed renderings of individual flowers from life for *The Language of Flowers*, published in 1884. The floral lexicon lists two meanings for sunflowers, "dwarf=admiration" and "tall=haughtiness."

TOP LEFT From Kate Greenaway, *The Language of Flowers*, 1884, and *Under the Window*, 1879 BOTTOM Walter Crane, *The Seasons*, late nineteenth century, oil on canvas
TOP RIGHT Walter Crane, "July and August," *King Luckie Boy's Party*, c. 1895 OPPOSITE Louis John Rhead, *Poster Calendar for 1897*, 1896, lithograph

Like their counterparts in Great Britain, American illustrators made inventive use of the sunflower's decorative form. It proved to be a popular image for journal covers and calendars, often as a symbol of high summer or evocation of the last vestiges of the season's bounty that survived fall's first chill. Here, a sleeping woman, dressed in a fanciful gown embellished with butterflies, is surrounded by towering sunflowers in full bloom. While the months represented—April, May and June— are not normally associated with the hearty flower, they bracket the season when the seeds are planted and the blossoms first appear. Thus, here spring seems to bring dreams of summer. But just as likely, the artist may have ignored the flower's actual season, selecting it rather for its natural, ornamental quality, easily translated into the flattened, formalized aesthetic and the pure, bright palette of commercial printing.

Wilde Flower

As icons of the Aesthetic Movement, the lily and the sunflower shed their traditional meanings

of purity and constancy. In quest of an art that existed for its own sake, advocates of the

movement advanced the daring thesis that an aesthetic experience was the sole reason to

pursue or appreciate artistic endeavor. In a lecture, "The English Renaissance" (1882), Oscar

Wilde, the articulate and self-appointed apostle of aestheticism, explained that aesthetes

favored the sunflower and the lily for the "gaudy leonine beauty of the one and the precious

loveliness of the other." These flowers, Wilde argued, were "the two most perfect models of

design" for the decorative arts in England. Walter Hamilton, in *The Aesthetic Movement

in England* (1882), was the first to devote a book-length study to aestheticism, and credited

Wilde with popularizing the lily and sunflower as hallmark motifs. Although Wilde himself had

taken on the lily as a signature flower, sporting it on his lapel and giving extravagant bouquets

of rare varieties to women he admired, the sunflower was thrust upon him by satirists in the

popular press. For satirists and cartoonists, Wilde, whose outrageous pronouncements

OPPOSITE *A Thing of Beauty Not a Joy Forever* (see p. 87) ABOVE *Oscar Wilde*, early 1880s, photograph

With his great height exaggerated by a tall, silk hat and a large lily embellishing his lapel, Oscar Wilde stands out, in the center right, among the celebrities portrayed in William Powell Frith's painting of a social gathering at the Royal Academy, London. Elegant women, including actresses Lily Langtry and Ellen Terry, press close to hear the words of the man Frith called "a well-known apostle of the beautiful," while, to the right, a group of men listen, their faces expressing some scepticism. At the far left, a woman is lost in reverie gazing up at an unseen work of art; the large sunflower on her bodice proclaims her an acolyte of aestheticism.

and unorthodox attire never failed to cause a sensation, appeared as spectacular and showy as the "gaudy" and "leonine" sunflower.

Born in Dublin, Wilde first rose to attention as a brilliant young scholar, winning literary prizes at Trinity College, Dublin, and Oxford University. While at Oxford, he transformed his rooms in Magdalen College into a showplace for his refined taste, featuring an eclectic display of antique furniture, oriental rugs, and export porcelain from Asia. Upon completing his education in

1879, Wilde moved to London, where he earned a reputation as a charming conversationalist armed with a razor-sharp wit. He exploited his great physical stature with an eccentric mode of dress, and he demonstrated his powerful talent for self-promotion through self-parody, with remarkable quips such as "I find it harder and harder every day to live up to my blue china." As an art critic and a lecturer, Wilde advocated the ideas of aestheticism, and soon his outlandish public image became inseparable from the excesses of the

TOP William Powell Frith, *A Private View at the Royal Academy*, 1881, oil on canvas   BOTTOM Linley Sambourne, *Caricature of Oscar Wilde*, from *Punch*, 1881

Aesthetic Movement. When his first collection of poems appeared in 1881, *Punch* artist Linley Sambourne caricatured him as a giant sunflower, with the caption declaring "The poet is WILDE, / But his poetry's tame."

From its inception, the Aesthetic Movement provided an easy target for parody in the pages of the humor journal *Punch*. An extravagant sunflower, drawn by Sambourne for the annual "Almanack" issue of 1877, opened the assault.

By the early 1880s, the sunflower was so strongly associated with the Aesthetic Movement that Mary Eliza Haweiss, whose column, "Beautiful Houses," appeared regularly in the journal *The Queen*, made the acid remark that "a blue pot and a fat sunflower in the window are all that is needed to be fashionably aesthetic." In the spring of 1881, *Patience*, a comic opera written by W. S. Gilbert and Arthur Sullivan, drew record crowds to Richard D'Oyly Carte's Savoy Theatre in London. "Bunthorne," the posturing protagonist, is a "fleshly poet" whose demeanor and dress reminded the public of Wilde. At the end of the year, the impresario D'Oyly Carte sent a touring company of *Patience* to New York; shortly after, he arranged for Wilde to give lectures in North America. Both men insisted that the two events were unrelated, but *Patience* created an enthusiastic audience for Wilde. In his signature velvet

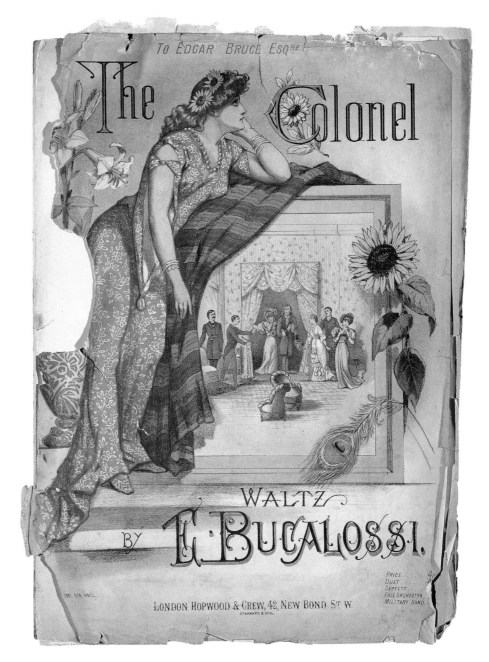

The play *The Colonel*, by J. C. Burnand, presents a gentle satire on aesthetic taste.

English music cover, *The Colonel Waltz*, 1881, color lithograph

suit, Wilde delighted the press as well; his image appeared everywhere, more often than not bearing a sunflower as an ensign of his aestheticism. Wilde's tour lasted eighteen months, with venues as far flung as Boston, Chicago, Montreal, and Toronto, as well as a notorious visit down a Colorado mine shaft.

When Wilde returned to London, he cut his long hair and adopted a more conservative wardrobe. *Punch* responded by running an advertisement for the sale of "the whole Stock-in-Trade . . . of a Successful Aesthete who is retiring from business," including an ample selection

In taking aim at the Aesthetic Movement, satirists fixed their sites on Oscar Wilde. While neither the figure cum teapot above nor the posturing aesthetes on the sheet-music cover below bears a physical resemblance to him, the sunflowers— as well as the paraphrase of his famous quip and the knickerbocker suits—link these parodies to Wilde's public persona.

of "dilapidated Sunflowers." Wilde continued to lecture on Aesthetic Movement design until the last years of the 1880s, when he channelled his energy into editorial work and writing plays. By then the rarified taste of the Aesthetic Movement had become commodified and commonplace, and *The British Architect*, a leading forum for advanced design, wryly observed, "If there is nothing else to illustrate the fact, the sickening repetition of the sunflower . . . would be enough to show how little the general public have yet derived from the increased study of art."

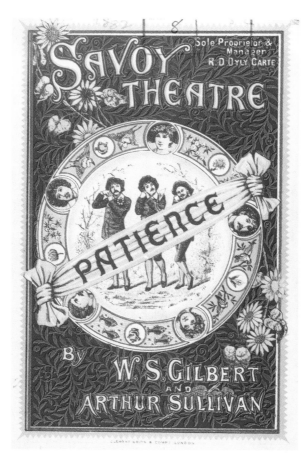

TOP Worcester Royal Porcelain Works, *Teapot* (inscribed "Fearful consequences through the laws of Natural Selection and evolution of living up to one's teapot"), 1882, painted porcelain BOTTOM Cover of program for Gilbert and Sullivan's "Patience," at the Savoy Theatre, London, 1881

"Well, let me tell you the reason we love the lily and the sunflower . . . is because these two lovely flowers are in England the most perfect models of design—the gaudy leonine beauty of the one and the precious loveliness of the other."

OSCAR WILDE, "Lecture on the English Renaissance," 1882

TOP Thomas Nast, "Mr. Wilde, You Are Not the First One That Has Grasped at a Shadow" and "Wilde on Us. Something to 'Live Up' to in America", *Harper's Bazaar*, 1882 BOTTOM Three pages from Charles Kendrick, *Ye Soul Agnies, in Ye Life of Oscar Wilde*, 1881

To demonstrate that the Aesthetic Movement craze had spun out of control, cartoonists caricatured aesthetes as limp-wristed, unhealthy, haggard, and posturing, prone to rapture at the sight of anything odd or exotic. While "Chinamania" and unintelligible poetry were just two of the many targets for mockery, the ubiquitous sunflower was the most recognizable symbol of aesthetic excess.

TOP F. W. Bell, *The Aesthetic Craze as Seen from a Chinese Point of View*, from *Harper's Bazaar*, 1882   BOTTOM *Ultra Christmas 1881*, from *Harper's Bazaar*, 1881

A THING OF BEAUTY NOT A JOY FOREVER.
Rise and Fall of a "Vera" Wilde Æsthete.

After his successful lecture tour of North America, Oscar Wilde returned to London, clipped his hair, and dressed in a more conventional manner. He also cut back his activity on the lecture circuit, redirecting his energies to writing and editorial work. Both the British and American press portrayed the change as a fall from celebrity, mocking Wilde as an Aesthetic has-been. This American cartoon contrasts Wilde at the height of his popularity, standing on a stage strewn with gold coins and illuminated by a radiant sunflower, with his supposed fall from fame, looking dull, shabby, and carrying a battered valise decorated with crude sunflowers, faded badges of his fleeting glory.

New York cartoon, *The Judge: A Thing of Beauty Not a Joy Forever*, 1883

Golden Gratitude

During the warmest days of August 1888, Vincent van Gogh wrote to his friend Émile Bernard that he was thinking of decorating his studio in Arles with paintings of sunflowers. He vividly described the chromatic effect he was seeking: "A decoration in which chrome yellow, crude or broken, shall blaze forth against various backgrounds—blue, from the palest malachite green to *royal blue*." Van Gogh had left Paris for Arles early that year, trading the dismal gloom of a northern winter for the warmth of the southern, Provençal sun. Snow-covered fields greeted his arrival that February, but an early spring coaxed the orchards into flower, and soon the fields were covered with wild iris and cultivated wheat. Van Gogh worked energetically to capture the glory of each phase of nature's flowering in pure color on canvas. Painting under the strengthening sun revitalized his health and spirit, but loneliness blunted the pleasure of his new-found home. Van Gogh had carried a deep, personal dream to Arles, to draw together a circle of kindred souls who would live and work communally as a "Studio of the South." When Bernard received van Gogh's letter, he had just joined Paul Gauguin in Pont-Aven in Brittany. Van Gogh

OPPOSITE Vincent van Gogh, *Fourteen Sunflowers in a Vase*, 1888, oil on canvas ABOVE Vincent van Gogh, *Self-Portrait*, 1886/87, oil on board

wrote wistfully that he wished to be there as well, but as he could not, he would try to "find consolation in contemplating the sunflowers."

While it is difficult to accurately reconstruct the origins of van Gogh's attachment to the sunflower, his family background and his Dutch cultural heritage must have contributed to the iconic potential he recognized in its bright color and radiant form. His father, Theodorus, was a Dutch Reform pastor, and both his parents were deeply committed to the teachings of the Groningen School, a reform Calvinist movement that advocated the imitation of Christ through acts of humility and service to the poor. Devoted to emulating Christ's example of humble self-sacrifice, pious practitioners reflected the actions of their redeemer in their own lives, following the path of Christ just as the sunflower follows the course of the sun. As a young man, van Gogh spent over a year, from May 1877 to July 1878, in Amsterdam, where he could have seen a number of buildings ornamented with carved sunflowers. He regularly visited the Trippenhuis, the home of

Vincent van Gogh, *Bowl with Sunflowers, Roses, and Other Flowers*, 1886, oil on canvas

the Rijksmuseum until 1885, to study the paintings of Rembrandt van Rijn and Frans Hals. Built in 1662, the Trippenhuis features a relief of sunflowers in the pediments above the first-story windows of its classical façade. He may have also taken note of decorations on the Felix Meritis building, headquarters of an association of wealthy Dutch citizens, founded in 1777 to promote the arts and sciences. Its motto, "Happiness through merit," is symbolized by an industrious beehive, flanked by a sunflower and a rose and illuminated by the rays of the sun.

In 1886, when van Gogh moved to Paris to live with his brother Theo, he was deeply involved in the study of color. To brighten his palette, he painted flowers,

Vincent van Gogh sketched this stand of sunflowers in Arles in 1888. Giant sunflowers were a common feature of local cottage gardens, and the artist enjoyed capturing the natural spectacle of their broad blooms carried aloft on towering stalks.

ABOVE Pieter Luypen, *Three Putti Holding the Emblem of Felix Meritis*, 1787, terracotta
BELOW Vincent van Gogh, *Garden with Sunflowers*, 1888, pen and ink on paper

assembling bouquets from the local market. The sunflower first appears in his work in this context, as a strong visual accent in a bowl of roses and other flowers. During the summer months of 1887, the artist took his easel to the semirural district on the outskirts of Montmartre, where many of the cottage gardens boasted sunflowers that towered above the trellises and sheds. He included these vigorous and commanding plants in sketches and paintings he made in the open air. Later that summer, he painted four studies of cut sunflower blossoms, concentrating on the rich variation of hue from pale citron to deep ocher and capturing the rustic vitality of the flower by modeling the ragged petals and twisted stems with heavy strokes of impastoed pigment.

Sunflowers also featured in the cottage gardens of Arles, and van Gogh imagined them as the perfect decoration for a house he had rented. Van Gogh hoped to transform the house, with its four rooms and a bright, yellow exterior, into a lively center for a brotherhood of artists. He drafted an invitation to Gauguin to join him at the Yellow House. Early that autumn, Gauguin sent an ambivalent response, promising to come at the first opportunity. In a state of expectant enthusiasm, van Gogh began to decorate a room for Gauguin, painting "great pictures of sunflowers, 12 or 14 to the bunch." Writing to his brother, van Gogh explained that he had to work quickly, "for the flowers fade so soon,

and the thing is to do them in one rush." He worked his paint with passion, often plying unmixed color with a heavy, expressive stroke. Late in September, with only four of the canvases completed out of the twelve he had planned to produce, van Gogh informed Theo that he wanted to paint more sunflowers but, because it was late in the season, "they were already gone." Gauguin had still not set his travel plans, and although van Gogh worried that the painter would not experience the beauty of a Provençal summer, he was convinced that paintings of the sunflowers would express the power of the vital summer sun.

Gauguin arrived near the end of October. Van Gogh was thrilled that his colleague appreciated his images of sunflowers, writing to Theo that his guest found them superior to similar subjects by Monet. Early in December, Gauguin painted a portrait of van Gogh in front of his easel, studying a resplendent bouquet of sunflowers in a cobalt-blue vase. This must have been a partly imaginary depiction, since by now the season for sunflowers had long passed. But the work indicates Gauguin's sensitivity to the importance of the motif for van Gogh. By this time, the relationship between the two men was irreparably frayed, and late in the month, when Gauguin claimed that van Gogh had threatened him with a razor, only to turn it on himself, Gauguin left Arles. After a stay in the hospital, van Gogh returned to the

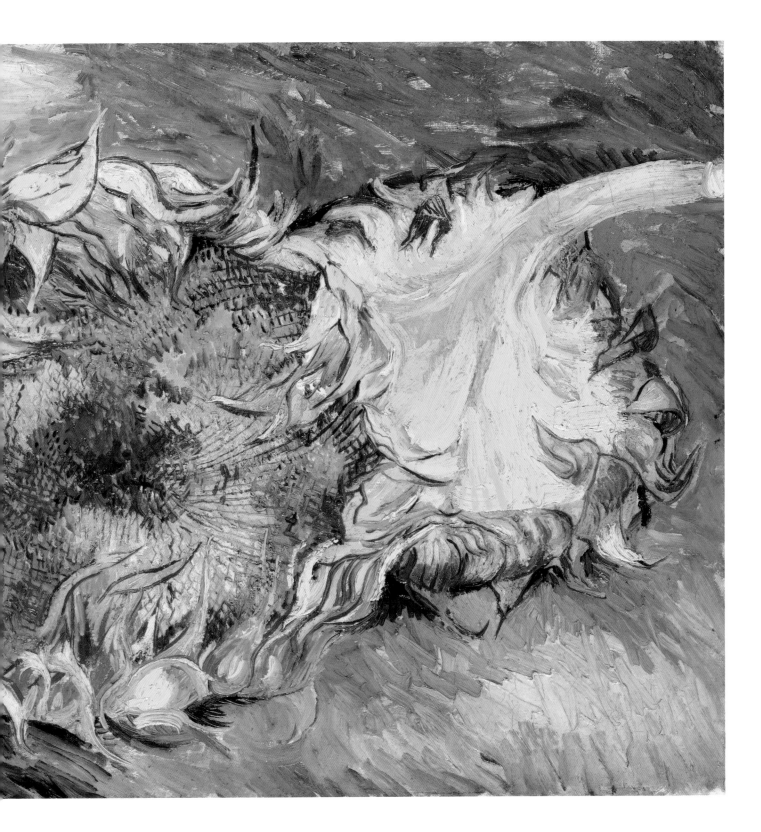

Vincent van Gogh, *Two Sunflowers*, 1887, oil on canvas

Gauguin was telling me the other day that he had seen a picture by Claude Monet of sunflowers in a large Japanese vase, very fine—but he likes mine better.

VINCENT VAN GOGH, letter to Theo van Gogh, 1888

In August 1888, Vincent van Gogh undertook his sunflower series, painting from freshly picked flowers in hopes of completing a dozen or more canvases. By the end of September, when the growing season ended, he felt forced to put the endeavor aside. The following January, after his hospitalization, he sought to make sense out of his shattered life and returned to the subject. Although he could not obtain sunflowers during the cold winter months, Van Gogh painted three bouquets, using his own paintings to stir his memories of the flower, which was out of season.

OPPOSITE Vincent van Gogh, *Sunflowers*, 1888, oil on canvas ABOVE Vincent van Gogh, *Vase with Sunflowers*, 1888, oil on canvas

Yellow House. In his letters to Theo, he reflected upon his bright bouquets, modestly asserting: "The sunflower is mine in a way." He painted three more sunflower bouquets that winter, using previous canvases as his models, but after that, the sunflower was absent from the artist's repertory. In a letter to his sister Wil in February 1890, van Gogh admitted that many of his pictures were a "cry of anguish," but "the rustic sunflower . . . may symbolize gratitude." Over the centuries, the sunflower had accrued many meanings: worship, devotion, constancy, and admiration. To them van Gogh added consolation and affirmation of a brief, golden moment in his art for which he always remained grateful.

TOP Vincent van Gogh, *Couple Strolling through Sunflowers on a Hill*, 1887, pencil on paper
BOTTOM Vincent van Gogh, *Vases with Sunflowers*, from a sketchbook, 1890, pencil on paper

Paul Gauguin, *The Painter of Sunflowers*, 1888, oil on canvas

Flowers for Vincent

On July 27, 1890, Vincent van Gogh walked out into a wheatfield where he had been painting since late May on the outskirts of Auvers-sur-Oise. He shot himself in the chest and died two days later. Upon receiving the news of the attempted suicide, Theo van Gogh rushed to Auvers, arriving at his brother's side just before his death. In a letter to his wife, Jo, Theo expressed gratitude for having been able to share the final moments of Vincent's troubled life. He praised the kindness of Dr. Paul Gachet, a homeopathic physician with equal interests in the arts and neurotic disorders, who had kept a sympathetic and watchful eye on van Gogh after he had left Provence in May to move to Auvers. Many artists who lived in the town attended van Gogh's funeral, and eight of his friends journeyed north to Auvers from Paris. But, Theo noted, Gachet was the first to arrive to pay his respects, bringing a "magnificent bunch of sunflowers because [Vincent] loved them so much."

Émile Bernard also attended the funeral, and he described the room that held van Gogh's coffin in a letter to the critic Albert Aurier. His last canvases hung on the walls, "making a kind of halo around him." Covering his simple coffin were "masses of flowers, the sunflowers he

OPPOSITE Roland Holst, catalogue cover for exhibition in Amsterdam of works by Vincent van Gogh, 1892, lithograph ABOVE Fernando Botero (p. 109)

loved, yellow dahlias, yellow flowers
everywhere. It was his favorite color, if
you remember, symbol of the light that
he dreamed of finding in hearts as in
art works." Aurier undoubtedly recalled
van Gogh's identification with the
golden color of sunflowers. He had
received a letter from the artist in
February, in response to an essay he

had written on the painter's work for
the journal *Mercure de France*. Van Gogh
thanked Aurier for his article, which he
declared to be "a work of art in itself,"
and debated some of the writer's observations of color theory, remarking that
the two sunflower canvases by him that
hung in the current exhibition of the
avant-garde art society Les Vingt in

Belgium "have certain qualities of
color," but "they also express an idea
symbolizing 'gratitude.'"

For van Gogh's friends, the sunflower now represented love and loss, a
golden tribute to the late painter, his
life-affirming love of nature, and his
passionate devotion to self-expression
in art. A vigorous sunflower provides

ABOVE Paul Gauguin, *Sunflowers on an Armchair*, 1901, oil on canvas OPPOSITE Émile Bernard (designer), *Decorative Panel with Flowers*, 1891–92, embroidered wool on linen

"Oh yes! he loved yellow, this good Vincent,
this painter from Holland—those glimmers of
sunlight rekindled his soul, that abhorred the fog,
that needed the warmth."

PAUL GAUGUIN, "Natures mortes," *Essais d'art libre,* 1894

the centerpiece for a set of decorative fabric panels that Bernard designed in 1891. Although not intended as a commemoration of the late painter, the panels capture the spirit of van Gogh's celebration of his signature flower. Bright in color, bold in form, the woven sunflower evokes the vitality of nature, beautiful for its regenerative power. In 1892 the artist Roland Holst organized a memorial exhibition, presenting 112 works by van Gogh in Amsterdam. Holst, a Dutch Symbolist influenced by the late painter, designed a lithograph for the cover of the exhibition catalogue. Van Gogh's emblematic flower is dry and drooping, with brittle leaves and ragged petals. But the radiant sun is seen in the distance, and the sunflower's blossom is crowned with a halo.

Paul Gauguin did not attend the exhibition, for in the spring of 1891, he had left France for Tahiti in quest of a simple, pure environment in which he could make his art and live in harmony with nature. He returned destitute two years later. While in Paris, he sought new patrons and dealers in hopes of raising the needed funds to return to the South Seas, and he directed his creative force into the completion of an

Inspired by deep, personal attachment, Émile Bernard and Paul Gauguin included sunflowers in their paintings and designs after Vincent van Gogh's death. The sunflower appeared in the work of artists of a new generation as well. The association between van Gogh and his signature flower was well known, and among those who admired his work, the sunflower served as a simple homage to an artist who remained constant to his own vision no matter the sacrifice.

illustrated manuscript that he called *Noa Noa*. The Polynesian title refers to fragrance, a lingering, perfumed scent that when inhaled triggers memory. *Noa Noa* conveyed Gauguin's sensory experience of his recent journey, but other writings of the time reveal that his thoughts strayed back to his deceased friend. In January 1894, the image of van Gogh's painted sunflower sent him into reverie: "In my yellow room, sunflowers with purple eyes stand out on a yellow background; they bathe their stems in a yellow pot in a yellow table. In a corner of the painting, the signature of the painter: Vincent . . . Oh yes! he loved yellow, this good Vincent, this painter from Holland—those glimmers of sunlight rekindled his soul, that abhorred the fog, that needed the warmth." Long after he returned to the South Pacific, Gauguin was haunted by van Gogh's memory; a number of his late still-life paintings include a bouquet crowned with one or more sunflowers.

Artists beyond van Gogh's circle also responded to his work, and the

James Ensor, *Flowers and Vegetables*, 1896, oil on canvas

In the decades immediately following Vincent van Gogh's tragic death, artists often depicted the sunflower—once a symbol of vitality—as faded or wilting.

sunflower was adopted as an icon of dedication and self-sacrifice in the pursuit of a deeply expressive and personal artistic vision. The Belgian painter James Ensor executed a modest still life of root vegetables and a drooping sunflower, echoing van Gogh's association of the flower with humble but essential labor on the land.

A leading early twentieth-century Austrian proponent of Art Nouveau, Gustav Klimt delighted, as van Gogh clearly did, in the intense hues and shapes of gardens with sunflowers, but, stressing their decorative potential, he incorporated them in expansive surfaces of intense pattern and color. To other artists, the thick, twisting stalks and broad, nodding heads of van Gogh's bouquets seemed to imbue the flower with an elemental physical force that suggests the visceral element of human emotion. German Expressionists recognized this biomorphic power and painted sunflowers of heartrending beauty. The deep, somber palette of Emil Nolde's oil painting of two ripe flowers bowed by the weight of their seeds, each

Georges Lemmen, *Sunflowers*, 1895, watercolor with pen and ink on paper

surrounded by an eerie halo of yellow, makes the blooms seem about to burst with the apocalyptic force of a volcano. Even among the formalist movements of the avant-garde, van Gogh's sunflower remained an icon: the French Cubist Georges Braque kept a reproduction of a sunflower painting by the nineteenth-century artist pinned to his studio wall. The Dutch painter Piet Mondrian, who became the leader of the De Stijl movement (which aimed to suggest the essence of nature through purified compositions of straight lines and primary colors), used realistic renderings of sunflowers as a point of departure for his early investigations into the abstract nature of form.

Long after van Gogh's death, artists continued to remember him with sunflowers. The Dutch painter Isaac Israëls paid homage to his fellow countryman's famous bouquets in a work of 1917, filling a canvas with his rendition of one of the series of still lifes by van Gogh, to which he added the partly visible figure of a female viewer. Sixty years later, the Colombian painter Fernando Botero referenced

While Gustav Klimt explored the inherent decorative quality of the sunflower, Piet Mondrian reduced it to its most essential formal elements. Other artists, such as Georges Lemmen and Emile Nolde found the flower possessed an expressive force, as if its broad, heavy head and tattered petals forged an analogue for the weary anguish of human emotion.

OPPOSITE Gustav Klimt, *Farm Garden with Sunflowers*, 1905–1906, oil on canvas
ABOVE Piet Mondrian, *Sunflower I*, 1907, oil on canvas

van Gogh's sunflower series in a still life of his own: featuring numerous sunflowers arranged in a vase similar to one that van Gogh used in his compositions, Botero's work includes a small painting of the motif standing on an easel. The painting within the painting seems to glow, imbuing it with an intensity not present in the still life behind it, as if to say that the beauty of actual flowers is fleeting but the work of art endures, in fact increasing in significance for future generations. As

recently as 1991, the American artist Faith Ringgold drew upon the same celebratory life force that van Gogh found in Provence in her jubilant quilt painting *The Sunflowers Quilting Bee at Arles*.

While the association of the sunflower with van Gogh inspired visual tributes throughout the twentieth century, diverse interpretations of the flower have secured its place in the modern artistic repertory. Georgia O'Keeffe concentrated on the yellow

corona of petals and enigmatic, dark center in a number of magnified studies of the bloom. For mid-century regionalist painter Charles Burchfield, the sunflower's lofty height and vibrant color embodied the vitality of agrarian America. The flower's distinctive form, so long regarded as an elemental expression of strong, natural design, could metamorphose into elegant frailty and translucent beauty through the lenses of accomplished photographers such as the American Edward

ABOVE Emil Nolde, *Sunflowers*, 1932, oil on canvas OPPOSITE TOP LEFT Isaac Israëls, *Woman in Profile in Front of van Gogh's Sunflowers (Homage to van Gogh)*, 1917, oil on canvas
OPPOSITE TOP RIGHT Fernando Botero, *L'Atelier*, 1977, oil on canvas OPPOSITE BOTTOM Dorothea Tanning, *Eine Kleine Nachtmusik (A Little Night Music)*, 1946, oil on canvas

Steichen and the Japanese Yasuhiro Ishimoto. Ishimoto calls his subjects *Common Sunflowers*, perhaps ironically, since there is nothing common about his breathtaking view of the flower's perfectly geometric center and the uplifting quality he achieved in a view of its head from below.

In 1946 the Surrealist Dorothea Tanning transformed the sunflower's benevolent image into a menacing force of gigantic size, with a fearsome head and writhing roots, in a depiction of the dark mysteries of a nightmare. And as recently as the last decade of the twentieth century, the German artist Anselm Kiefer portrayed sunflowers in advancing states of decay in his prints and used dried stalks and seeds in his assemblages, as if to remind the viewer of the ephemeral nature of existence. In the 1998 sculpture *Horus*, he combined sunflowers and books: two of van Gogh's favorite motifs. The dried flowers spring dramatically from the lead volumes as if from the earth, dramatically signaling the cycle of life and death, as did the ancient god whose name this work carries. Horus was a falcon-headed figure whose eyes, the Egyptians believed, were the sun and the moon.

Thus the long tradition endures, each interpretation adding a layer of meaning to the strong, stately sunflower. Its vitality is revealed in its rich cultural history, nourished by the artistic imagination as well as by the annals of science; issues of faith; and intriguing tales of myth, legend, and lore.

TOP Charles Burchfield, *Sunflower Row*, c. 1942, watercolor   BOTTOM Faith Ringgold, *The Sunflowers Quilting Bee at Arles*, 1991, acrylic on canvas with pieced fabric border
OPPOSITE Anselm Kiefer, *Horus*, 1998, steel bookcase with lead books and dried sunflowers

Yasuhiro Ishimoto, *Common Sunflower*, 1986–87, photograph

Arber, Agnes. *Herbals: Their Origin and Evolution, A Chapter in the History of Botany 1470–1670*. London: Cambridge University Press, n.d.

Aslin, Elizabeth. *The Aesthetic Movement: Prelude to Art Nouveau*. New York, Praeger, 1969.

Baker, Margaret. *Discovering the Folklore of Plants*. Princes Risborough, Buckinghamshire: Shire Publications, 1996.

Comito, Terry. *The Idea of the Garden in the Renaissance*. New Brunswick: Rutgers University Press, 1978.

Druick, Douglas W., and Peter Kort Zegers. *Vincent van Gogh and Paul Gauguin: The Studio of the South*. Chicago, Amsterdam, New York, and London: The Art Institute of Chicago, Van Gogh Museum, and Thames & Hudson, 2001.

Gere, Charlotte, and Lesley Hoskins. *The House Beautiful: Oscar Wilde and the Aesthetic Interior*. London: Lund Humphries, 2000.

Goody, Jack. *The Culture of Flowers*. Cambridge University Press, 1993.

Grierson, Mary, and William T. Stearn. *An English Florilegium*. New York: Abbeville Press, 1987.

Hamilton, Walter. *The Aesthetic Movement in England*. London: Reeves and Turner, 1882.

Hedrick, U. P. *A History of Horticulture in America to 1860*. Portland, Oregon: Timber Press, 1988.

Heiser, Jr., Charles B. *The Sunflower*. Norman: University of Oklahoma Press, 1976.

Hyam, Roger, and Richard Pankhurst. *Plants and Their Names: A Concise Dictionary*. New York: Oxford University Press, 1995.

Jill, Duchess of Hamilton, Penny Hart, and John Simmons. *The Gardens of William Morris*. London: Frances Lincoln Ltd., 1998.

Johnson, Lady Bird, and Carlton B. Lees. *Wildflowers across America*. New York: Abbeville Press, 1988.

Kenseth, Joy. *The Age of the Marvelous*. Hanover: Hood Museum, 1991.

Lambourne, Lionel. *The Aesthetic Movement*. London: Phaidon, 1996.

Mancoff, Debra N. *Van Gogh: Fields and Flowers*. San Francisco: Chronicle Books, 1999.

Pavord, Anna. *The Tulip*. London: Bloomsbury, 1999.

Powell, Claire. *Meaning of Flowers, a Garland of Plant Lore and Symbolism from Popular Custom and Literature*. Boulder, Colorado: Shambhala, 1979.

Russell, Vivien. *Monet's Garden: Through the Seasons at Giverny*. London: Francis Lincoln Ltd., 1995.

Schaap, Ella B. *Dutch Floral Tiles in the Golden Age*. Haarlem: Becht, 1994.

Seaton, Beverly. *The Language of Flowers: A History*. Charlottesville, University Press of Virginia, 1995.

Silverman, Debora. *Van Gogh and Gauguin: The Search for Sacred Art*. New York: Farrar, Straus, and Giroux, 2000.

Sitwell, Sacheverell, and Wilfrid Blunt. *Great Flower Books 1700–1900*. New York: The Atlantic Monthly Press, 1990.

Swan, Claudia. "*Ad vivum, naer het leven, from the life: defining a mode of representation,*" *Word and Image* 11, 4 (October–December, 1995). Pp. 353–72.

Vickery, Roy. *Dictionary of Plant Lore*. Oxford: Oxford University, 1997.

Ward, Bobby J. *A Contemplation upon Flowers: Garden Plants in Myth and Literature*. Portland, Oregon: Timber Press, 1999.

Whittemire, Katharine. "How a Weed Once Scorned Became the Flower of the Hour," *Smithsonian Magazine* 27, 5 (August 1996). Pp. 52–61.

ACKNOWLEDGMENTS

Every author draws upon the expertise and support of colleagues and friends, and I would like to take the opportunity to acknowledge those who helped this endeavor at every stage. First and foremost, I would like to thank Peter Kort Zegers, Rothman Family Research Curator at The Art Institute of Chicago, whose work on the exhibition "Van Gogh and Gauguin: The Studio of the South" revealed the fascinating scope of the sunflower's cultural history. Without Peter's initiative, imagination, and vast archive of information, this book would never have been written. Thanks go as well to Amanda W. Freymann, for organizing and overseeing the project, Joan Sommers for her beautiful design, Susan F. Rossen for her expert editing, Stacey Hendricks for her assistance, and Carol Parden for her picture research. I would also like to express my gratitude to the staff of the Ryerson and Burnham Libraries at the Art Institute, notably Peter Blank, Jack Perry Brown, Lauren Lessing, Martha Neth, and Susan Perry; and colleagues at the museum, including Karen Altschul, Judith Barter, Barbara Hind, Kristin Lister, Adrienne Jeske, Bernd Jesse, Barbara Mirecki, Britt Salvesen, and Mary Weaver, for their assistance and encouragement. Thanks go as well to Sarah Gordon for her work at the early stage of this project, and to Audrey Druick, Paul F. Gehl, Elinor R. Mancoff, Philip Mancoff, and Anatole Upart for their contribution to this endeavor.

D. N. M., Chicago, Illinois, May 2001

PHOTO CREDITS